40
FASCINATING
Conversion
STORIES

D1024150

Books by Samuel Fisk

Forty Fascinating Conversion Stories

More Fascinating Conversion Stories

40 FASCINATING Conversion STORIES

Compiled by
SAMUEL FISK

kregel
PUBLICATIONS

Grand Rapids, MI 49501

Forty Fascinating Conversion Stories compiled by Samuel Fisk.

Copyright © 1993 by Kregel Publications.

Published in 1993 by Kregel Publications, a division of Kregel, Inc., P.O. Box 2607, Grand Rapids, MI 49501.

All rights reserved. No part of this book may be reproduced, stored in a retrieval system, or transmitted in any form or by any means—electronic, mechanical, photocopy, recording or otherwise—without written permission of the publisher, except for brief quotations in printed reviews.

Editorial Assistance: Helen Bell
Cover and Book Design: Alan G. Hartman

Library of Congress Cataloging-in-Publication Data

  Fisk, Samuel.
Forty fascinating conversion stories/by Samuel Fisk.
    p.   cm.
  1. Conversion. 2. Protestants—Biography. I. Title.
BX4825.F58   1993   348.2'4'0922—dc20 92-39338
                                      CIP

ISBN 0-8254-2639-1 (pbk.)

3 4 5 Printing/Year 97 96

Printed in the United States of America

CONTENTS

FOREWORD

"For the greatest and most regal work of God is the salvation of humanity."
—*Clement of Alexandria, c. 220 A.D.*

All believers have a story to tell—a story of forgiveness and grace, a story of how God's provision in Jesus Christ met the deepest needs of the human heart. And if our Lord's parables of the lost coin, the lost sheep, and the lost sons tell us anything, it is that each life and each story is highly significant to the Father and the occasion for "joy in the presence of the angels of God."

To remember and to celebrate the conversion of those men and women who achieved some degree of recognition in Christian service, therefore, is not to suggest that their individual conversions are of greater worth or their subsequent acts of service merit higher reward than the repentance and obedience of those whose service in the Kingdom will never be known this side of heaven. To paraphrase Tertullian, it is the blood of the martyrs—not their press clippings—that is the seed of the Church.

There are, however, good and godly reasons for a book such as *Forty Fascinating Conversion Stories*. The first is to demonstrate that the good news of God's saving work in Jesus Christ really is what the Apostle Paul called it in his letter to the Roman Christians: "the power of God unto salvation to every one that believeth." It is the power of the Gospel that transformed the wretched trafficker in slaves into the author of "Amazing Grace." The Good News of Jesus Christ so transfigured individuals that love

9

for Christ could send a Goforth to China, a Livingstone to Africa, or a Taylor to China.

It was D.L. Moody who, in response to the debate challenge of the famed agnostic Robert Ingersoll, agreed on the condition that Ingersoll produce one person whose life had been lifted from degradation by the power of agnosticism. Moody, for his part, promised to produce dozens who had been saved from the deepest levels of despair by the Gospel message. Samuel Fisk has here documented another two score to add to the number.

There is also something to be said for a compilation of such testimonies as a "witness" in the sense of sworn testimony before a court in which one offers evidence, a common theme in the New Testament. In an age of relative value systems and the exaltation of the subjective, the historic message of the Gospel is that it changes lives because it is true, because Jesus is indeed the Truth which can be known and can liberate.

Conversion stories demonstrate not only the truth but also the power of that truth to change an individual, a society, and the course of human history. They remind us of the value of A.A. Trites's comments on the importance of Christian witness:

> The frequent use of the witness-theme in the New Testament stresses the importance of the historical foundation of the Christian religion. The claims of Christ as the Son of God are currently widely disputed. In such an environment a brief must be presented, arguments advanced and defending witnesses brought forward, if the Christian case is to be given a proper hearing. To fail to present the evidence for the Christian position would be tantamount to conceding defeat to its opponents.[1]

Forty Fascinating Conversion Stories is a brief, a deposition, a transcript of testimony that challenges us to witness boldly for the Lord of changed lives.

Grand Rapids, MI   DENNIS R. HILLMAN, Senior Editor
                               Kregel Publications

---

1. "Witness, Testimony," *The New International Dictionary of New Testament Theology*, Vol. 3 (Grand Rapids: The Zondervan Corporation, 1978), 1047-48.

1

SIR ROBERT ANDERSON:
Head of Scotland Yard

S ir Robert Anderson was so successful as an English police inspector that he became head of the famous Scotland Yard from 1888–1901. He was knighted by Queen Victoria and made Knight Commander by King Edward VII. Yet he is most well-known for his books on Bible truth, especially his writings on prophecy and eschatology. His volume *Human Destiny* was long a standard work on the after-life. For more than a century his books have been reprinted over and over again.

The story of his conversion as told here by his son is from *Sir Robert Anderson, a Tribute and Memoir*, by A. P. Moore-Anderson.

The son relates: "The story of my father's conversion to God is told in the *Life of Faith* (a British magazine). He had been brought up in a Christian home and had led what is known as a religious life, with occasional transient fits of penitence and anxiety; but the conversion of one of his sisters through services held in Dublin [where they were living at that time] awakened new spiritual longings. He was persuaded to accompany her to one of these meetings; but the light came the following Sunday evening through a sermon in his own church. The preacher was the Rev. John Hall (afterwards of New York), who 'boldly proclaimed forgiveness of sins, and eternal life as God's gift in grace, unreserved and unconditional, to be received by us as we sat in the pews. His sermon thrilled me,' Sir Robert continues, 'and yet I deemed his doctrine to be unscriptural. So I waylaid him as he left the vestry, and on our homeward walk I tackled him about his heresies. At last he let go my arm and, facing me as we stood upon the pavement, he repeated with great solemnity his gospel message and appeal: "I tell you," he said, "as a minister of Christ and in His name, that there is life for you here and now if you will accept Him. Will you accept Christ or will you reject Him?" After a pause—how prolonged I know not—I exclaimed, "In God's name I will accept Christ." Not another word passed between us; but after another pause, he wrung my hand and left me. And I turned homewards with the peace of God filling my heart.'

"In the aftermath of the Irish Revival, lay preaching became a recognized institution. Of my father's introduction to the work he tells these words: 'One afternoon, soon after my conversion, I received a letter from a friend telling me he was unable to keep an engagement to address a gospel meeting and asked me to fill his place. His messenger waited for the answer, and I promptly replied that I could not take such a position. But then I remembered I had been praying that God would give me work to do for Him; might not this be the answer to my prayer? So I hurried after the messenger to tell my friend of my change of mind. And the next day I preached my first gospel sermon.' A preaching tour in the South of Ireland followed in the year in which he left college."

And Robert Anderson was on his way!

Taken from the book, *The Life of Sir Robert Anderson* by A.P. More-Anderson. Copyright © 1947 Marshall, Morgan, & Scott, Ltd. Used by permission of HarperCollins Publishers, London.

2

WILLIAM BOOTH:
Founder of the Salvation Army

In sixty years of active ministry, William Booth, founder of the Salvation Army, preached over sixty thousand sermons and recruited and deployed two million soldiers for his Army in fifty-five countries of the globe.

From a poverty stricken home where his father had died while he was a child, William Booth rose to receive worldwide recognition. Though an Englishman, he was asked to deliver the opening prayer in the United States Senate in 1898. He was "the first Christian leader to be received as such by the Japanese Emperor." With little formal education, an honorary degree was conferred upon him by Oxford University. He inspected and encouraged his Army workers in Germany, Palestine, Australia, New Zealand, and other lands "on every continent and the islands of the sea."

But such recognition did not come easily. He was criticized by the rich and abused by slum dwellers. When, with his early corps of workers he began preaching in front of saloons and dens of vice, mobs of ruffians and drunks were instigated to disrupt and, if possible, stop the efforts. Booth and his workers often returned to their quarters with bloodied faces and rotten egg-spattered uniforms. But they kept right on. In various places gangs sprung up "composed of the worst hooligans of the district, who, primed with drink, followed and brutally ill-treated the defenseless Salvationists. Magistrates withheld police protection. Salvationists were blamed, frequently sent to prison and fined, for breaches of the peace caused entirely by their enemies" (Religious Tract Society).

A recent Associated Press dispatch declares, "Mocking hedonists once pelted them with live coals or dead cats as they sang outside saloons. At least they were noticed. Today, Salvation Army officers complain of public apathy over their preaching."

Not only did interests of vice oppose him, but Booth's religious methods were so contrary to the stolid and staid ways of the Church of England, prominent prelates and their partisans openly denounced him. Lord Shaftesbury fumed that the Salvation Army was "a trick of the devil . . . trying to make Christianity ridiculous." But, as did a number of notables, Queen Victoria met him, and her successor, Edward VII, helped further balance the score. When invited to the palace to be presented to the King, Booth was granted the unusual privilege of being allowed to wear his Salvation Army uniform and cape instead of the usually required formal frock and coat; and equally unusual was the Monarch's shaking him by the hand (almost never done) as he said, "You are doing a good work, a great work." No wonder a statue of Booth now stands at the sight in East London where his soul-winning and relief work began.

But before Booth (or anyone else) could preach a saving message to others, a salvation experience had to be real for him. Harold Begbie in his *Life of General Booth* characterized Booth's experience thus: "No conversion could be simpler, less dramatic, and more natural; few in the long history of Christianity have brought a richer harvest to the world." Earlier Begbie says, "This headstrong and impulsive boy determined to make that total and mysterious surrender of personality which is a condition precedent to what we call conversion."

Turning to an account published by the Religious Tract Society (London), we read: "In his early boyhood there was no religious influence in his life, no restraining hand upon his tendencies, and no attempt of any kind to shape or mold his character. He developed a fiery temper and impetuous will, formed his own ideas, sought adventure with the most spirited boys of his acquaintance, and took the lead in every game and device for killing time. . . . The almost sudden death of his father made a deep impression on his mind, and from that time William Booth began to take an interest in religion. It was not long before he discovered in the atonement of Jesus Christ all he needed to satisfy his own soul's needs."

Other aspects of the story come out in a life of General Booth by C. T. Bateman: "A chance visit to a Wesleyan chapel induced him to relinquish the services of the Church of England and become a regular worshipper with the Wesleyan Methodists. Methodism attracted and touched those deep chords of religion in his nature. Conversion and salvation were the truths emphasized by the workers at this chapel. William Booth came under this direct influence. He was arrested by the thought of his guilt and the need for salvation. To him this experience, even though a lad still in his early teens, was real and tangible; it gripped him."

At this point it may be well to let Booth speak for himself. As do a number of biographers, we take up the story in his own words. "Many of my companions were worldly and sensual, some of them even vicious. . . . One feeling specially forced itself upon me, and that was the sense of the folly of spending my life in doing things for which I knew I must either repent or be punished in the days to come . . ."

Then came the famous incident of the pencil-case. "The entrance to the Heavenly Kingdom was closed against me by an evil act of the past. In a boyish trading affair I had managed to make a profit out of my companions, while giving them to suppose that what I did was all in the way of a generous fellowship. As a testimonial of their gratitude they had given me a silver pencil-case. Merely to return their gift would have been comparatively easy, but to confess the deception I had practiced upon them was a humiliation to which for some days I could not bring myself.

"I remember, as if it were yesterday, the spot, the hour, the resolution to end the matter, the rising up and rushing forth, the finding of the young fellow I had chiefly wronged, the acknowledgment of my sin, the return of the pencil-case—the instant rolling away from my heart of the guilty burden, the peace that came in its place . . .

"Since that night when the happy change was realized, the business of my life has been to live a life of loving activity in the service of God and man. I have ever felt that true religion consists in assisting my crucified Lord in His work of saving men and women . . ." And later, "A new set of feelings took possession of my soul. I was converted, and with all the force of which my nature was capable I gave myself up to seeking and saving the lost".

These last sentiments expressed may need underscoring today in view of the increasing emphasis being placed on strictly humanitarian "welfare work," whereas originally the Salvation Army's efforts in that direction actually grew out of recognizing the salvation of the soul being the true basis of the surest help to man. Bateman's biography declares Booth's interests thus: "Never once did he abandon the theology expressed by 'conversion.' He taught it in the Army by means of the penitent-form, and no meeting was completed, according to his conception, that did not include an invitation to the sinner. Who shall say that the constant and pervasive recognition of this religious principle did not serve as the greatest factor in his world-wide evangel? . . .

"He expressed a passion for souls. His journal contains constant references to 'the necessity of laboring for the salvation of souls,' or similar phrases, coupled with particulars of results. He was preaching then, as he always did, for definite conversion."

Others confirm this emphasis. The afore cited Begbie says, "History will show that he grew into humanitarianism, and that this humanitarianism was the developed fruit of his religion." And Kerr and Mulder (in their "Conversions") speak of his work "in terms of evangelism and social relief. Booth never wavered from insisting that saving souls came first . . ."

And a more up-to-date witness is found in *Eerdman's Handbook to the History of Christianity*, where we read, "The Salvation Army was concerned about spiritual rather than material conditions. Booth spoke out against attempts to deal with great social difficulties as though they were simply due to lack of bricks and mortar. The first thing to be done to improve the condition of the wretched was to get at their hearts." May these highest priorities ever be embraced.

A few points regarding Booth's funeral (1912) illustrate the recognition which finally came to him. So great was said to be the press at his "lying-in-state" that it had to be extended to three days while 150,000 filed past. Then came the funeral in the vast London exhibition hall where 40,000 crowded in. A *Reader's Digest* article (February, 1965, p.302) reports, "Unknown to most, royalty was there too. Far to the rear of the hall, almost unrecognized, sat

Britain's Queen Mary, a staunch admirer of Booth. She had elected to come at the last moment without warning."

Next to the Queen, on the aisle, sat a former fallen woman, now saved. As the casket moved slowly up, this woman reached out and placed three beginning-to-fade carnations on the casket, which remained to the end of the service, the only flowers on it. As Queen Mary turned, perhaps with an enquiring look, the girl said simply, "He cared for the likes of us."

3

William Borden:
Ivy League Hero of Faith

William Borden seemed to have everything going for him in life—the envy, or what might be dreamed of, by most young people. Abundant wealth, physical robustness, intellectual brilliance, a popular personality, ability to lead, and yet not spoiled in the least by any of these, he radiated above all a deep and abiding consecration to Christ, finally giving his very life to make Him known.

A popular book among young people—and many others—during the late twenties and well beyond was *Borden of Yale '09* by Mrs. Howard Taylor. So great has been the interest that a reprint was brought out for the '80s.

The biography begins with the words, "When the death of William Borden was cabled from Egypt, it seemed as though a wave of sorrow went around the world. There was scarcely a newspaper in the United States that did not publish some account of a life which had combined elements so unusual . . ." (p. ix). Who could imagine a young man in his middle twenties calling forth tributes from "the House of Commons in London" to "the National Parliament in Peking (China)" (p. 275)?

In his student days Borden could slip away from his well furnished campus accommodations to either city dwelling or seaside estate, both maintained by servants, to find quiet retreat or entertain friends sumptuously. But he demonstrated an all-round manhood when on his private yacht he would replace the captain, take over the helm, climb aloft to handle the rigging, work at repairing the engine, or cook and serve a meal to his guests.

Intellectually brilliant he was a top scholar throughout university and graduate study (president of Yale's Phi Beta Kappa), an outstanding athlete—from football, baseball, tennis, wrestling (few were ever able to pin him down), to the winning varsity rowing crew. Full of fun, he appreciated a prank and frequently engaged in a dorm "rough house." Another side: he found time to keep up with the *New York Times* and the *Wall Street Journal* (maybe he felt the need as he managed the family estate for his widowed mother and younger sister).

Popular, he was elected to so many responsible offices which he filled with distinction it made people wonder where he found time to study and maintain a position at the head of his class—yet his life was so given to God he would never study on Sundays! He started every day, Bible in hand, with his quiet time (guests or no guests to look after), and he was faithful in a number of weekly prayer circles, some of which he himself started. While a student at Yale he founded and maintained a downtown rescue mission. He was a great personal worker.

He kept up the same high standards throughout Princeton Seminary days (mastering several ancient languages), although taking a break to attend by appointment and fully participate in the great Edinburgh Missionary Conference of 1910. Dr. Samuel M. Zwemer, associate of his Cairo days, wrote, "Here was a man with the frame of an athlete, the mind of a scholar, the grasp of a theologian as regards God's truth, and the heart of a little child, full of faith and love" (op. cit., p. 240).

Young Borden displayed such sane and balanced judgment, such organizing and administrating ability, and such deep consecration that (among other things) he was appointed, while still in seminary, a trustee of the Moody Bible Institute of Chicago; a director of the National Bible Institute of New York—and chairman of their building committee; and a member of the North American Council of the China Inland Mission (the largest faith mission of that day). Dr. James M. Gray, head of Moody Bible Institute, asked him to prepare a statement for the doctrinal standards of the Institute.

Borden's ordination in the Moody Church of Chicago "gave the daily papers a good deal to say," one Chicago daily presenting "an account of the proceedings that must have arrested attention, printing in full on its front page" the hymn so appropriately used for the occasion ("When I Survey the Wondrous Cross") (ibid. p. 209).

While young Borden was unstintingly generous, giving many thousands of dollars to Christian work, he never wanted any personal credit for it, often giving it anonymously. One associate termed him, "a general in organization, but always willing to be a private in service" (ibid., p. 229).

Borden was not only willing to give time and means to missions, he did not hold back his very own life, pressing on to service in one of the most difficult fields of the world—Moslem missions in northwest China. His first step on the way was to study Arabic and Islamics in Cairo. Here he suddenly came down with a fatal illness. But his life was not wasted; the impress of it lives on.

The biography contains considerable reference to his mother and reveals the strong influence for good she had upon his life.

And what was the beginning of the all-pervading hold that God had on Borden's life? Nothing sensational, just a simple yielding to the claims of the gospel.

The biography relates, "When William was about seven years old, Mrs. Borden entered upon a new experience spiritually which was deeply to affect his life. A devoted mother before, she now became an earnest, rejoicing Christian. To her, Christ was real and fellowship with Him, satisfying in no ordinary degree." She became active in the Moody Church, Chicago. "The result was very evident in the life of her younger son, who owed the strength and grasp of his spiritual convictions largely to that church home."

"It was there he took his first step in open confession of Christ. Seated by his mother one Sunday morning, he heard Dr. Torrey, then pastor of the church, give the invitation to the communion service about to be held.

"'Is it not time that you were thinking about this yourself, William?' his mother whispered.

"'I have been,' was the unexpected reply.

"'When the elements were handed from pew to pew, to Mrs. Borden's surprise, William quietly took the bread and wine as did those about him. Rather taken aback at this interpretation of her question, Mrs. Borden mentioned the matter to Dr. Torrey who smiled and said, 'Let him come and see me about it tomorrow.'

"Young though he was, his answers to Dr. Torrey's questions made it evident that he was ready for the step he had taken, and the interview led to his joining the church in the regular way."

Before entering college, while making a round-the-world tour, Borden again heard Dr. Torrey, this time in London, and wrote home to his mother, "Dr. Torrey spoke about being 'born again,' and mentioned some of the foolish ideas people have about it. His sermon was meant to straighten things out. I know my own ideas were somewhat hazy, and I wasn't at all sure about it. But I am now. The text was John 3:6, and Dr. Torrey gave five proofs by which we can tell whether we are 'born again,' born of the Spirit or not . . . So we have only to believe in Jesus and receive Him, and immediately we have power to become sons of God."

The result for Borden was sure, and many have since had reason to thank God for it.

4

JOHN A. BROADUS:
Great American Theologian

The life of John A. Broadus should be of special interest to Baptists, but others should by no means be disinterested. I was told quite a number of years ago that Broadus' commentary on the Gospel of Matthew was regarded by some as the greatest single volume commentary ever published in the English language. I have used it many years with real profit. And his Preparation and Delivery of Sermons has been for many, many years a standard textbook on homiletics in both Baptist and other schools.

A write-up in *Christianity Today* (April 13, 1962), says, "Broadus' preaching, teaching, and writing were destined to influence and change countless lives, far beyond his own lifetime. It has been said of his text *Preparation and Delivery of Sermons* that 'No other work in the field of homiletics has had so wide and extended use in the history of theological education.' . . . Demands for Broadus to speak in churches of all evangelical denominations multiplied."

The same article relates an early experience during Civil War days. A general "sent special couriers with notice that Dr. Broadus would preach, and an immense crowd of probably 5,000 attended, General Lee . . . among them . . . Hundreds came forward to ask for prayer or profess a new-found faith . . . Seeking opportunities for witness, he also would distribute tracts in hospitals."

The recent (1982) *Wycliffe Biographical Dictionary of the Church* gives fair place to Broadus, pointing out that he was, "For a time assistant professor of Latin and Greek at the University of Virginia," and that later, upon the Southern Baptist Theological Seminary becoming established in Louisville, Kentucky, he was designated its president. This source further mentions, "Attained high rank as teacher, preacher, and scholar. Published notable books."

V. L. Stanfield, compiling a volume of his sermons, says, "During the last half of the nineteenth century in America, no Baptist preacher enjoyed greater popular fame than did John A. Broadus . . . In 1889, he gave the Lyman Beecher Lectures on Preaching at Yale University, the only Southern Baptist ever to be accorded this honor" (written about 1959).

And how did this noteworthy man experience Christ? The story is told in his biography, by his equally distinguished son-in-law and successor, Archibald T. Robertson, *Life and Letters of John Albert Broadus* (Philadelphia, 1901).

We read, "There was no overseer that winter, and the boy, not yet fourteen, had charge of the farm, the saw mill, and everything while Major Broadus [his father] was away . . . He learned to split rails, to plow, to mow, to bind wheat, to rake hay, to pull fodder, and everything else necessary on the farm. He worked with the men as well as managed the farm . . . On the long winter nights and rainy days he kept up his Latin, reading largely . . ."

A year later: "One day John came home from school with his trunk. Major Broadus feared he had been expelled, and asked for an explanation. John solemnly said: 'My uncle [the teacher] says he has no further use for me.' His father could get no more out of him, and went over to see Mr. Simms, who laughed and said that John had learned all that he could teach him."

Finally the life-determining day came. "While he was still at school, a protracted meeting was conducted at Mt. Poney Church, Culpeper, by Rev. C. A. Lewis and Rev. B. Grimsley. Mr. Broadus was converted at this revival. While under conviction and feeling unable to take hold of the promises, a friend quoted to him: 'All that the Father giveth me shall come to me; and him that cometh to me I will in no wise cast out' (John 6:37), repeating 'in no wise cast out.' 'Can't you take hold of that, John?' Somehow the light dawned under this verse of Scripture."

A close friend wrote later: "We were youths of about the same age . . . Our fathers had been opposing candidates for the legislature. In May, 1843, at a protracted meeting, conducted at Culpeper, we both professed conversion, joined the church the same day, and were together baptized in Mountain Run, just above where the bridge crosses the stream . . . In our little debating societies and prayer meetings he was always clear and logical in his statements, and devout in his supplications."

Roberston continues the story. "In a meeting a few months after John's conversion, the preacher urged all Christians at the close of the service to move about and talk to the unconverted. John looked anxiously around to see if there was anybody present he could talk to about his soul's salvation. He had never done anything of the kind before. Finally he saw a man, not very bright, named Sandy. He thought he might venture to speak to him at any rate; and Sandy was converted. John soon went away to teach school. Whenever he came back Sandy would run across the street to meet and say: 'Howdy, John; thankee John.' Dr. Broadus often told of this first effort of his at soul winning and would add: 'And if ever I reach the heavenly home and walk the golden streets, I know the first person to meet me will be Sandy, coming and saying again: 'Howdy, John; thankee, John.'"

And that was not the last person Broadus pled with to come to Christ. Note how he closed some of his sermons with heart-felt appeal:

Concluding one: "O my friends, what is your relation to Jesus? It is the question of all questions: what is your relation to Jesus? It is a question which you should settle in your honest heart . . . O my friends, what is your personal relation to Jesus? It is a question which you can postpone now, if you will, but you will face it in the day for which all other days were made; in the day when before the Savior you will stand, and He your judge . . . O my friends, prepare for that day by turning to Christ now! What is your personal relationship to Jesus? Confess Him now!"

One more: "Whosoever will. As if carefully guarding against all misunderstanding, anyone who will is invited to come . . . Here, here only, whosoever will may take, whosoever will shall surely receive. Whosoever will . . . whosoever will . . . Many things call you away—but oh, heed the invitation of the text. And make up your mind that you will come to Christ."

5

JOHN BUNYAN:
Immortal Author of Pilgrim's Progress

Warren Wiersbe declares *Pilgrim's Progress* "the most popular Christian classic ever produced in the English-speaking world." And V. Raymond Edman, late president of Wheaton College, tersely stated, "John Bunyan, though bound with chains for preaching the truth of God, was in spirit free. Like Paul also, Bunyan's writings have lived through the centuries, and wherever the Bible has gone in hundreds of translations, Bunyan's *Pilgrim's Progress* has followed." Then, speaking of its leading character's entrance "into the city of the Great King," Edman says, "By many it is regarded as the finest piece of writing in the English language, as well as a magnificent presentation of spiritual truth."

Coleridge, a literary master himself, declared, "I know of no book, the Bible excepted, as above all comparison—which I, according to my judgment and experience, could so safely recommend." And of another great literary scholar we read, "In his famous essay upon Bunyan, Macaulay pays this tribute to his genius: 'That wonderful book, while it obtains admiration from the most fastidious critics, is loved by those who are simple . . . The style of

Bunyan is delightful to every reader, and invaluable as a study to every person who wishes to obtain a wide command over the English language. There is no book in our literature . . . which shows so well how rich that language is' . . ."

In view of the tributes cited, it is a remarkable fact that Bunyan had almost no formal schooling, certainly no advanced education. He was a God-molded man. Traveling about as a tinker after he came to know Christ, he was simply burdened to tell anybody and everybody, whenever and wherever possible, about the mighty Savior, and increasingly crowds hung on to his words. This popularity put him in conflict with the established church and eventually led to his twelve years of wretched imprisonment since he was unyielding in his personal convictions.

The noted British author, Froude (a twelve-volume English history, numerous biographies of great men, etc.), wrote a full life of Bunyan pointing out that he was never formally tried, he refused a pardon for conscience sake and, as Froude says, his imprisonment "might have ended at any time if he would have promised to confine his addresses to a private circle." He left behind a dependent wife and four small children—one blind, who died while he was in prison—and the good wife suffered a miscarriage over the shock of his arrest and inability to secure his release. Had he yielded to demands, he might have ministered to thousands in approved churches, but, instead, what he wrote in prison has ministered to millions through untold years when his voice has long been silent.

Both by word of mouth and in his voluminous writings, Bunyan bore witness to a great deliverance in his life. As to the precise point of his conversion, biographers have found it difficult to pinpoint for he wrote a whole volume, *Grace Abounding*, on his rather turbulent religious development.

The established church could not meet the needs of a man like Bunyan. Froude says, "To a man of fervid temperament suddenly convinced of sin, incapable of being satisfied with ambiguous answers to questions, the church of England has little to say. If he is quiet and reasonable, he finds in it [the church] all that he desires. Enthusiastic temperaments demand something more complete and consistent."

As a youth, Bunyan seemed at times deeply convicted over his spiritual state. While apparently not involved in grosser sins, he confesses to periodic burdens over worldly frivolities, dancing, lying, Sabbath-breaking, and blaspheming the Name of God. One source says, "He was morbidly sensitive to sin; he was tormented by dread of reprobation; he thought his day of grace was ended." Then he would swing over to indifference, then the consciousness of this would only increase his miserable state. In his despair he would think the devil had him in his grasp.

Bunyan's numerous biographers draw attention to two or three incidents or trials in his life which helped him come into the full truth of God and mark his conversion.

Showing how at one point Bunyan recognized his need, he says, "One day as I was standing at a neighbour's shop window, and there cursing and swearing, and playing the madman after my wonted manner, there sat within the woman of the house and heard me, who, though she was a very loose and ungodly wretch, yet protested that I swore and cursed at the most fearful rate, that she was made to tremble to hear me; and told me further that I was the ungodliest fellow for swearing that she had ever heard; and that I, by thus doing, was able to spoil all the youth of the whole town. At this reproof I was silenced and put to secret shame, and that too, as I thought, before the God of Heaven. As I stood there hanging down my head I wished with all my heart that I might be a little child again; for, thought I, I am so accustomed to it, that it is in vain for me to think of reformation."

Soon after the woman's rebuke he fell in "with a poor man who made profession of religion and talked pleasantly of the Scriptures." So Bunyan studied "the Bible and began to take pleasure in reading it."

Even more commonly recounted is this notable occasion: "Upon a day, the good providence of God called me to Bedford, to work at my calling, and in one of the streets, I came where there were three or four poor women sitting at a door in the sun, talking about the things of God; and being now willing to hear them discourse, I drew near to hear what they said. Their talk was about a new birth, the work of God on their hearts, also how they were convinced of their miserable state by nature. They talked how God had visited their souls with His love in the Lord Jesus, and with what words and promises they had been refreshed, comforted, and supported against the temptations of the devil, and how they had borne up under his assaults. They also discoursed of their wretchedness of heart and of their unbelief. And I thought they spoke as if joy did make them speak; they spoke with such pleasantness of Scripture language, and with such appearance of grace in all they said, that they were to me as if they had found a new world. I left them and went about my employment again, but their talk and discourse went with me; also my heart would tarry with them, for I was greatly affected with their words."

A subsequent occasion seems to vouchsafe the crowning point of Bunyan's assurance. He recounts, "One day, as I was passing in the field, and that too with some dashes on my conscience, fearing lest yet all was not right, suddenly this sentence fell upon my soul, *Thy righteousness is in heaven*; and I saw with the eyes of my soul Jesus Christ at God's right hand, there, I say, as *my* righteousness; so that wherever I was, or whatever I was doing, God could not say of me, *He wants my righteousness*, for that was just before Him. I also saw, moreover, that it was not my good frame of heart that made my righteousness better, nor yet my bad frame that made my righteousness worse, for my righteousness was Jesus Christ Himself, 'the same yesterday, and today, and forever.'

"Now did my chains fall off my legs indeed. I was loosed from my afflictions and irons, my temptations also fled away; now went I also home rejoicing for the grace and love of God."

In *The Life of John Bunyan*, by Wm. Henry Harding, we read, "In all those weary months of zigzag he gradually approached the glorious goal. His ideal was a definite conversion, a spiritual regeneration: 'I did see such glory in a converted state that I could not be contented without a share therein. Had I a whole world, it had all gone ten thousand times over for this.'"

We conclude with the words of Dr. Edman, "His neighbors and friends were aware of a great change in his life and urged him to preach the Word to them and to others. He was timid so to do, but then was persuaded that God had given him the ministry of preaching and teaching."

Thank God for John Bunyan!

6

WILLIAM CAREY:
Father of Modern Missions

William Carey (1761-1834) has long been acknowledged as "the father of modern missions," the man who sparked the effort in the era in which we live to reach out with the gospel to the ends of the earth. The story of his life is not only interesting, it is amazing.

While apprenticed as a young shoemaker, Carey learned Latin, Greek, Hebrew, French and Dutch, and while still in his teens could read the Bible in six languages. He was the instrument that initiated the epoch of modern missions. He saw the Bible, or sizable portions thereof (six completely), translated and published "in about 40 Oriental languages or dialects, besides a great number of tracts and other religious works in various languages," including grammars and dictionaries (Funk & Wagnalls *New Standard Encyclopedia*). He advanced native agricultural industries, medical relief, schools and colleges, steam machinery, and printing presses. He led in the abolition of casting infants into the sacred Ganges and the burning of widows upon the cremation pyres of their husbands.

In *The New Acts of the Apostles*, A. T. Pierson says: "For ten years he bore the brunt of sneer and taunt, and the worst hostility of inertia and indifference; felt the keen sting of Sidney Smith's wit and sharp rebuke of John Ryland's hyper-Calvinism. But when a saint gets on his knees and sees God's signals flashing—floods and flames cannot stay his progress. Between the Scylla of apathy and the Charybdis of antipathy, Carey boldly steered for India. While others slept, he dared not falter or delay; he must move, though he moved alone."

In his history, The Progress of World-Wide Missions, R. H. Glover reports of Carey, "Resolved to fit himself for higher service, he utilized every available moment for classical study and wide reading, and by dogged perseverance, perhaps even more than by brilliancy of intellect, he mastered" the five languages referred to, "and gained a good knowledge of Botany and Zoology. A copy of Cook's 'Voyages,' which fell into his hands, made a deep impression upon him, leading his thoughts and sympathies out to distant lands, and a profound conviction laid hold upon him of the greater duty and task of the church to carry the gospel to the heathen world. Before him in his cobbler's stall hung a large map of the world . . ." The story has often been retold.

Not Baptists alone, who might naturally be thought to be proud of their fellow Baptist, but many from other groups (like Glover just quoted) have paid high tribute and acknowledged indebtedness to Carey. Let us note a few others.

In the Church of England, W. Wilson Cash stands high. In his *The Missionary Church* (London, Church Missionary Society, 1939), we read, "William Carey published in 1792 *An enquiry into the obligations of Christians to use means for the conversion of the Heathen.* In this remarkable treatise Carey traversed a wide sweep of history. He called special attention to the needs of South America, New Guinea, and many parts of Asia, of New Zealand (of which he had read in Captain Cook's book), and of Africa . . . His famous maxim has inspired men ever since: 'Attempt great things for God; expect great things from God.' A year later Carey sailed for India to lead the way in the great crusade of the Gospel in Asia . . . It was the arrival of Carey which ushered in a new day . . . The policy developed by Carey and others was that every missionary should be an evangelist. In those days it was in fact unthinkable for anyone to be a missionary who was not a keen evangelist; unfortunately, since then there has been serious loss to the Church of evangelistic work."

Finally, that eminent Presbyterian, Robert E. Speer in his *Missionary Principles and Practice,* reports, "It was out of prayer and revival that Carey and his little band of Baptist ministers addressed themselves to the task of evangelizing the world. Further still, the London Missionary Society was founded as a direct result of William Carey's work . . ."

Illustrative of how Carey confronted situations is the following, early in his ministry in India (from *Missionary Illustrations,* by A.C. Bowers, F. H. Revell Co., 1937):

"Carey, as he was returning home in a boat one day, saw a crowd of people gathered around a pile of wood near the edge of the water. Looking more carefully he noticed that there was a dead body laid on the wood, and as he went closer, he saw that they were preparing to burn the living wife of the dead man with him. He had known of this practice of *suttee,* but had never seen it done. In spite of his very earnest urging that they not carry through the terrible, cruel sin, they said to him that if he did not wish to see it he could go away. He pleaded with the young widow to refrain from the sin of suicide, but in reply she danced and laid down beside her husband. When she had placed her arms around his neck, his relatives piled leaves and branches over them, poured a large amount of melted butter over it all, and then tied two large bamboos on top to hold all down. Then the son of the dead man set fire to the heap. And Carey records that if there were any sound from out of the leaping flames, the shouts and singing of the crowd drowned them. From that time one of the great purposes of Carey's life was to root out the terrible custom of *suttee* . . . During the thirty-three years it required for him to bring about this one reform, at least seventy thousand women had been burned alive in Bengal."

And how did this great man come to know Christ in such a real way? We draw the story principally from two sources, *William Carey,* by Russell Olt (Warner Press), and the well-known biography by F. D. Walker (various editions).

Early influences left their mark. From Olt: "Through family and church training he acquired considerable familiarity with the Scriptures. His attention was absorbed mostly by the historical parts. He knew the prayer book, but the lack of evangelical tone in the teaching of the church made him only passively religious. He did, however, develop, as a result of his training, a despising of those who were at variance with the established church, the Dissenters [or 'Nonconformists'] . . .

"Early after starting his apprenticeship [as a shoemaker] he grew weary of a religious profession which was unsatisfying, and he became more careless and indifferent, even choosing doubtful companions as his associates."

Walker underscores these influences and carries them on. "A simple piety pervaded that cottage home. Edmund and Elizabeth attended church with scrupulous regularity and took their children with them. At home they possessed a Bible and used it. Bibles were not numerous in the villages in those days, for the British and Foreign Bible Society had not been thought of and Scriptures were expensive for humble folk. 'From my infancy I was accustomed to read the Scriptures,' wrote Carey in later years.

"It is only to be expected that the child of such a pious home would, even in boyhood, be the subject of some religious impressions. It is best to relate his religious experience in his own words: 'In the first fourteen years of my life I had many advantages of a religious nature, but was wholly unacquainted with the scheme of salvation by Christ. During this time I had many stirrings of mind occasioned by my being often obliged to read books of a religious character, and having been accustomed from my infancy to read the Scriptures . . . Of real experimental religion I scarcely heard anything till I was fourteen years of age; nor was the formal attendance upon outward ceremonies, to which I was compelled, a matter of choice.'

"We can picture him sitting with his school fellows in the parish church on Sundays . . . When the sermon ended with a solemn 'amen' from the clerk, the boys would prepare for release and lose no time in escaping through the porch to the village green. William was now approaching the 'troublesome age' at which so many boys become restless and desirous of throwing off the restraints of home. He said, 'I was addicted to swearing, lying, and unchaste conversation . . .'

"But for William Carey this period was only one of transition. He had already drunk too deep of purer fountains to be able to quench his soul-thirst at the village horse pond. His home training, his own inclinations, and the grace of God already working in his boy heart (though he knew it not) made it impossible for him to be satisfied with a life of ungodliness. For a brief while he looked the pleasures of sin in the face, and then he deliberately turned away from them with disgust and loathing."

Olt relates the deepening crisis: "It was at this point that an older fellow apprentice came to his rescue. John Warr was three years older and a young man who knew God. Moreover, he loaned him worthwhile books. William had little use at this time for Dissenters, but the effect of this personal evangelism was to cause him to determine to leave off lying, swearing, and other sins and attend church more frequently."

Nevertheless, young Carey misappropriated a shilling and then lied about it but, to his shame, was detected. Olt continues: "His offense was forgiven him by his master (likely through the influence of a newly married wife). The incident not only taught William a lesson but it directly changed his profession of religion for an experience of it. So at the age of seventeen and a half years he yielded himself to the Savior. To the personal evangelistic effort of his fellow apprentice, John Warr, more credit should be given than to any other person."

Walker brings out some of the underlying elements in the struggle : "Young Carey looked upon Dissenters with disdain, and long and heated were the arguments they had . . .

"Those workshop discussions appear to have been chiefly about heart religion as against formal observance. What in those days was often termed 'experimental religion' may not have been altogether a new idea to William, but now the subject was pressed upon his attention. The waywardness of recent years troubled him. He began to experience 'a growing uneasiness, the stings of conscience were gradually increasing'; and a heart-hunger took possession of him."

In the Dissenters' meeting place "Carey's proud spirit was deeply impressed and his views were, almost imperceptibly, undergoing a change. His soul was thirsting for God."

A final and complete surrender to God came about as a result of a meeting with Dissenters. Olt gives it briefly: "A novice at preaching pleaded for a whole-hearted surrender to Christ, quoting the words, 'Let us go forth, therefore, unto Him without the camp, bearing his reproach,' in such a gripping way that Carey was brought to the turning point in his thinking—a decision to join the ranks of the Dissenters."

Carey was soon found going about preaching the gospel. The story has often been told of how one day a friend stopped him and said, "Mr. Carey, I want to speak to you very seriously."

"Well, what is it?" Carey said.

The friend replied, "By your going about preaching as you do, you are neglecting your business. Attend you business more and you will soon get on and prosper, but as it is you are simply neglecting your business."

"Neglecting my business!" said Carey, looking at him steadily, "My business is to extend the Kingdom of God; I only cobble shoes to pay expenses."

We may well conclude with the telling words of A. T. Pierson: "With little teaching, he became learned; poor himself, he made millions rich; by birth obscure, he rose to unsought eminence; and seeking only to follow the Lord's leading, himself led on the Lord's host. Carey had passion for souls, and, therefore, enthusiasm for missions. Self-denial was his habit, and all the accumulations of his life in India were turned to the cause of God."

7

FANNY CROSBY:
Blind Visionary for Christ

Fanny Crosby is recognized as one of the most popular hymn writers of all time. Who is not familiar with "Blessed Assurance," "Safe in the Arms of Jesus," "Rescue the Perishing," "Saved By Grace" and others of her compositions? It is said she wrote over 9,000 hymns (Hefley, Sandville), "more than eight thousand of them appearing in print" (Lillenas). I find that Charles Wesley, the great British hymn writer, is reported to have published 4,100 hymns and to have left 2,000 in manuscript. E.K. Emurian is authority for the statement that Fanny Crosby has "written more hymns, songs and poems than anyone else since the beginning of the Christian era"!

Yet Fanny Crosby (Mrs. Alexander Van Alstyne) did not begin writing hymns until the age of forty-four. Even more remarkable is the fact that she was totally blind, having lost her sight through a tragic doctor's error at the age of six weeks. And her father died before she was one year old.

In spite of blindness, she often referred in her hymns to the sight which she was denied but which she anticipated when she would be released from mortal ties. How many of us when singing "Blessed Assurance" recall that it was one blind who exclaimed, "Visions of rapture now burst on my sight"? And looking forward by faith she could say, "Oh, the soul-thrilling rapture when I view His blessed face, and the luster of His kindly beaming eye; . . ." Or, "I know I shall see in His beauty the King in whose law I delight; . . ." And we cannot leave out, "And I shall see Him face to face, And tell the story—Saved by grace."

Some of her most appreciated hymns were written within the time of an hour or less. One day William H. Doane from Ohio came to her door and, when admitted, hurried over to her and said, "Fanny, in forty minutes I must catch the train to Cincinnati, and I need a new song for a great Sunday school convention there." After discussing it he said, "Thirty minutes left." She turned to her desk and after a bit handed him a paper, telling him to read it on the train. It turned out to be what many regard as her greatest hymn, "Safe in the Arms of Jesus." It was played by the band at the funeral of General U.S. Grant.

On a number of occasions, as with "Safe in the Arms of Jesus," Fanny was asked to listen to a tune by such composers as Doane or Ira D. Sankey and frame words to fit the music, which she did most acceptably.

Her poetic gift manifests itself in early published volumes of verse before she wrote hymns. She soon became widely recognized, meeting President James K. Polk in the White House, and speaking before the U.S. Congress in words that glorified her Savior. She traveled in many parts of the country, lecturing or giving Chautauqua talks and ministering at Christian conferences, as she did for D. L. Moody and others. She lived to be ninety-five.

After her testimony became appreciated, she visited slum missions where her words were eagerly received. Sensing the need in such places, she often frequented the missions and on one occasion after a young man was converted wrote "Rescue the Perishing."

The following story of her conversion is taken from her *Memories of Eighty Years* (Hodder & Stoughton edition, London, 1908):

"Turn to the class meeting at the Eighteenth Street Methodist Church. Some of us used to go down there regularly, and on Thursday evening of each week a leader came from that church to conduct a class in the Blind Institution. In those days I was timid and never spoke in public when I could possibly avoid it. I attended meetings and played for them on the condition that they should not call on me to speak.

"One evening the leader brought a young man with him who was destined to have an important influence in my life. He was a Mr. Camp, a teacher in the city schools and a man noted for his generous public spirit. I found him a true friend. We used to attend the class meetings together, but he never urged me in religious matters. And yet I owe my conversion to that same friend, in so far as I owe it to any mortal. By a strange dream I was aroused—not that the dream had any particular effect in itself except as a means of setting me to thinking. It seemed that the sky had been cloudy for a number of days, and finally (in the dream) someone came to me and said that Mr. Camp desired to see me at once. Then I thought I entered the room and found him very ill.

"'Fanny,' he asked, 'will you meet me in Heaven?'

"'Yes, I will, God helping me,' I replied; and I thought his last words were, 'Remember you promise a dying man!' Then the clouds seemed to roll from my spirit, and I awoke. I could not forget those words, 'Will you meet me in Heaven?' and although my friend was perfectly well, I began to consider whether I could really meet him or any other acquaintance in the Better Land, if called to do so.

"The weeks sped on until revival meetings were being held in the Thirtieth Street Methodist Church. Some of us went down every evening. On two occasions I sought peace but did not find the joy I craved until one evening it seemed to me that light must indeed come then or never; and so I arose and went forward alone. After prayer, the congregation began to sing the grand old hymn:

Alas, and did my Saviour bleed,
And did my Sovereign die?

And when they reached the third line of the fourth stanza,

Here Lord, I give myself away,

my very soul was flooded with celestial light. I sprang to my feet, shouting "Hallelujah!" and then for the first time I realized that I had been trying to hold the world in one hand and the Lord in the other.

"The next Thursday evening I gave a public testimony at our class meeting. I promised to do my duty whenever the dear Lord should make it plain to me.

"Not many weeks later, Mr. Stephen Merrit asked me to close

one of our class meetings with a brief prayer. My first thought was, 'I cannot'; then the voice of conscience said, 'But your promise!' and from that hour I believe I have never refused to pray or speak in a public service, with the result that I have been richly blessed."

8

M. R. DE HAAN:
Founder of Radio Bible Class

For a number of years I have had, on my shelf, volumes by the venerable Bible teacher, Dr. M. R. De Haan. These are only some of the 25 volumes he authored (not counting hundreds of small pocket editions of his radio messages). Indeed, it was not his books for which he was best known, but for his widely listened-to Radio Bible Class.

Little wonder, then, that when Dr. De Haan, not long before his death as it turned out, was to speak in our area (far from his home base), we went to hear him personally. His gravelly voice was very much the same, and so also the no-nonsense approach in his message, but a warm, tender personality shone through. It is said that three years before his death, Dr. De Haan, in two months, traveled more than 8,000 miles in his speaking ministry.

Dr. De Haan is rightly called "doctor" for, before his ministry in the gospel, he had gone through medical school and established a successful practice as a physician. Although he was the youngest in his class, he had graduated as valedictorian from the University of Illinois Medical School. Answering the call of God to the gospel ministry at the age of 30, he switched from presiding at the birth of babies to preaching the new birth. Among medical experiences, one is related where he performed an appendectomy in a country farmhouse, by kerosene lamp, the patient on the kitchen table.

But the change to a second career meant another educational stint—preparing himself in a theological seminary. Then followed his pastoring two churches in Michigan.

What has been regarded as his third career was his establishing the Radio Bible Class, over which he presided for 27 years, along with his writing ministry. His radio outreach soon grew to cover the continent from coast-to-coast over the Mutual network, and in such faraway places as Australia.

As to his books, Dr. Lehman Strauss reported from Korea that a local pastor told him he had never been privileged to attend seminary, "But," said he, "I received a seminary course from Dr. De Haan" in translating and preaching from his helpful books." Also, although often enduring ill health, Dr. De Haan had a wide ministry in Bible Conferences throughout the country and at places like the Moody Institute's Founders Week Conferences.

For the story of his conversion we turn to *M. R. De Haan, The Man and His Ministry*, by James R. Adair (copyright 1969 by Zondervan Publishing House, used by permission):

"There came a day when, at least to Martin, it seemed that God's hand had touched him in a special way. The slow clop, clop of horses' hoofs and the creaking of a buckboard wagon moving into town from the west and carrying a tall woman evangelist brought swarms of young Hollanders to Main Street, Martin among them. The woman came from the City Mission in Holland, Michigan, preaching a coming judgment on those not found in Jesus Christ, with clear statements on how to escape God's wrath:

"'Salvation is all of God's grace. You don't earn it by baptism, catechism, or church membership. You don't inherit it from your parents. Confess your sins and be born again by Jesus Christ into the family of God!' . . .

"She shook a long index finger at the Zeelanders, hoping the Truth would sink deeply into the hearts of some of her listeners. It was when he was about 12 that Martin felt singled out as the worst sinner in town. That day he didn't jeer with the rest of the kids, neither did he let on to anyone that the message had spoken to him. But as the buckboard creaked back toward Holland, with Nellie's husband at the reigns, he trudged homeward, serious, important thoughts bombarding his boyish mind and heart. Sometime that afternoon, likely in his room, 12-year-old Martin talked to God as never before. By faith he wanted to be saved and be the kind of Christian Nellie talked about.

"He apparently didn't discuss it in detail with his parents or friends, nor rush out to tell his pastor. This he felt was personal—between God and him. And, besides, those he knew would have thought him presumptuous to talk about being saved. Most good church-going Hollanders of that day hoped they were saved, but they didn't think anyone could know for sure. It is not clear that Martin had a genuine spiritual experience at this time; no marked change came into his life, though in later life he made occasional reference to the happening . . .

"It is well known that some people, facing death, see their past deeds flash before them. There's no written record of what transpired in the mind of 30-year-old Martin De Haan, M.D., as he struggled for life in October, 1921, in a Grand Rapids hospital. But it is known he did considerable thinking about his past—and about his future.

"For all of his 30 years he had been identified with the church. As a boy he had gone regularly; and even in medical school he had been faithful in attendance. In Byron Center he and Priscilla had joined the Reformed Church, and he had attended when he could. But his life hadn't been counting for God as it should have. There were sins in his life at which God's finger was pointing. He felt condemned, though as a 12-year-old boy he had presumably settled his relationship with God.

"Nurses passed silently in the hallway outside his room as a quiet transaction took place in the heart and life of the patient from Byron Center. Again, there is no record of the conversation he had with God. He never made a point of telling and retelling the experience. But he penned these words: 'I was born in 1891 of the flesh, "a child of wrath even as others." After a life of sin for 30 years I was born again of the spirit in October, 1921. Since then my only hope and aim is to exalt Him to whom be all glory forever and ever. Eph. 1:7.'

"Mrs. De Haan, who learned of his spiritual experience when she visited him in the hospital shortly after it happened, recalls that as he talked about it afterward he mentioned that he wasn't sure that he had truly met God at age 12. The hospital experience was a spiritual struggle. 'Spare my life and I'll serve You,' Dr. De Haan pleaded with God. And evidently he meant it with all his heart, for, after he went home a few days later and soon resumed his practice, God rode with him . . .

"Neighbors noticed the difference. The De Haans were among the few families who owned a phonograph, and, according to a longtime resident of Byron Center, 'When the windows were open we could hear such songs as "Since Jesus Came Into My Heart."'

"Farmers in their fields, and children at play, and even his horses, must have wondered what had happened to Doc, for from time to time Mrs. De Haan accompanied him on house calls and then enjoyed glad songs of the faith as they rode along like a honeymooning couple in the buggy. 'He had such joy in his heart that he liked to sing about it,' recalls Mrs. De Haan.

"It wasn't only knowledge of sins forgiven that made Doc burst with joy. This was enough, to be sure. But the idea that at 30 he was going to serve God brought great delight to him. When Martin told his mother the news, she wept with joy. God had answered her prayers concerning her son's waywardness. De Haan gave much credit to his mother for what had happened. 'I was blessed with a godly, praying mother, and her admonitions have never left me. I can still close my eyes and in memory see her kneeling at her bed, wiping the tears from her eyes with her blue checkered apron. It was Mother's prayers which influenced me more than all the preaching to which I was exposed with unfailing regularity."

Taken from the book, *M.R. DeHaan, The Man and His Ministry* by James R. Adair. Copyright © 1969 by Zondervan Publishing House. Used by permission of Zondervan Publishing House.

9

CHARLES E. FULLER:
Old-Fashioned Revivalist

For many years the Christian world knew the name of Charles E. Fuller as well—if not better—than that of any living Christian leader. His Old-Fashioned Revival Hour was listened to the world around, wherever the English language was known. He is credited with being instrumental in bringing the Gospel story to more people than any other individual up to that time.

A copy of the following incident was long carried in the wallet of Arthur W. McKee, the song leader at the time of Mr. Rader's meeting—so significant, as it turned out.

"Back in 1917 I was a successful young businessman from a Christian home, but I had my faith in God shattered in college.

"One Sunday in that year—and by the way it was the third Sunday in July—I went, out of curiosity, to hear Paul Rader preach at the Church of the Open Door in Los Angeles City. I entered the place a lost sinner; I came out under deep conviction because Paul Rader preached Christ and Him Crucified in such a spirit-empowered message that I saw myself a lost, undone sinner. He preached from Ephesians 1:18, 19.

"Leaning my head on the seat in front of me I trembled under deep conviction, though I did not then know what was the matter with me. I left the afternoon meeting and drove out to a park in Hollywood, where I got down on my knees in the back of my touring car, and there, in prayer after a real struggle, I asked God to save my soul, which He did—and to use me in some capacity to reach others for Himself.

"I became a new creation, then and there, and I went back to the evening meeting to hear Paul preach another sermon, which seemed to me like manna from Heaven. My heart was fairly bursting with joy, and all desire to get ahead in the business world and to make money left me. I just wanted God to use me, if He could, to win souls for Himself.

"Later I had blessed fellowship with Brother Paul in conference work in McPherson, Kansas, and in Indianapolis. He wrote his name in a Bible which I use constantly, and beneath it he wrote, 'Days of Heaven on earth.' Truly our days of fellowship together in those conferences were heavenly days.

"I wish to say that I, with other thousands of souls, will look him up in Glory and say, 'Brother Paul, I'm here because the Holy Spirit used the Word of God as you gave it forth to bring me under conviction, and to save my soul.'"

10

JONATHAN GOFORTH:
God's Man in China

Jonathan Goforth was a truly apostolic character. He towers as a spiritual giant among God's missionary heroes of his generation, yet he would be the last person to take any personal credit for his wonderful successes in China. Hundreds if not thousands of persons generally professed conversion in each place he went.

While revival fires kindled in Goforth's field in China, he was asked to minister in Korea and the Holy Spirit was poured out in like manner.

Ralph Connor (Charles W. Gordon), author of such high-minded novels as *The Sky Pilot*, was a classmate of Jonathan Goforth in Canada. After Goforth's death he wrote, "The characteristic features of Goforth were the utter simplicity of his spirit, the selfless character of his devotion, and the completeness of his faith in God. I came more and more to honor his manliness, his humility, his courage, his loyalty to his Lord and his passion to save the lost . . . The grace of God in him made him the great man, the great missionary, the great servant of Jesus Christ that he was."

And also upon his death the *Moody Monthly* referred to Goforth as "this widely honored and beloved servant of the King, whose testimony has sounded with the clearness and sweetness of a silver bell for full half a century. The hand of God was upon Goforth in a mighty way."

We take the story of Goforth's conversion from *Goforth of China* by his consecrated and devoted wife, Rosalind Goforth. She begins with what Jonathan himself wrote: "From earliest years I wanted to be a Christian. When I was seven years of age a lady gave me a fine Bible with brass clasps and marginal references. This was another impetus to search the Scriptures. One Sunday, when ten years old, I was attending church with my mother. It was communion Sunday, and while she was partaking of the Lord's Supper, I sat alone on one of the side seats. Suddenly it came over me with great force that if God called me away I would not go to Heaven. How I wanted to be a Christian! I am sure if someone had spoken to me about my soul's salvation I would have yielded my heart to Christ then."

But for more than eight years he was left in uncertainty. Mrs. Goforth continues the story: "Jonathan Goforth was now getting on in his eighteenth year. He was known as a 'good lad, diligent, always ready to help others, eager to get an education (though this seemed, at times, hopeless), and he was liked by all for his happy, friendly ways'—but he was still an unawakened soul."

Jonathan attended a local school at which a Rev. Mr. Cameron sometimes spoke. Desiring to hear the kindly clergyman in his own church, Jonathan began attending services. Continuing the biography we read: "One who was present at that first Sunday gives the following. 'Almost sixty years have passed since then, but I can still see the young stranger sitting immediately in front of the minister with an eager, glowing look on his face and listening with great intentness to every word of the sermon.'

"It was Mr. Cameron's unvarying custom to close each sermon with a direct appeal for decisions. We give in Jonathan's own words what took place the third Sunday under Mr. Cameron: 'That Sunday Mr. Cameron seemed to look right at me as he pled, during his sermon, for all who had not, to accept the Lord Jesus Christ. His words cut me deeply and I said to myself, "I must decide before he is through." But contrary to his usual custom, he suddenly stopped and began to pray. During the prayer the devil whispered, "Put off your decision for another week." Then immediately after the prayer, Mr. Cameron leaned over the pulpit and with great intensity and fervor again pled for decisions. As I sat there, without any outward sign except to bow my head, I yielded myself up to Christ.'

"How complete was that yielding can be seen by his after life, and also from the following dictated to a daughter on his seventy-fifth birthday: 'My conversion at eighteen was simple but so complete that ever onward I could say with Paul, " . . . Christ liveth in me, and the life which I now live in the flesh I live by the faith of the Son of God who loved me and gave Himself for me.""'"

Another said of Goforth, "When he found his own soul needed Jesus Christ, it became a passion with him to take Jesus Christ to every soul."

Through sickness and hardship in China, the Goforths saw five precious children at various ages die and be buried in that inhospitable land. They went through the horrible Boxer Uprising, but enduring great suffering where other missionaries lost their lives, God brought them safely through.

Mr. Goforth was asked to participate in a great missionary convention in Washington, D.C. (January 28 to February 2, 1925). In a large volume containing the proceedings, with opening address by President Calvin Coolidge, Mr. Goforth's message is presented, in which he said in part, "Thirty-seven years ago I went to China, firmly believing that the Lord Jesus Christ could and would win the Chinese to Himself . . . I have preached the gospel depending upon the Holy Spirit to make it all powerful. At the story of God's love in Christ Jesus I have seen people convicted and converted . . ."

Taken from the book, *Goforth of China* by Rosalind Goforth. Copyright Bethany House Publishers. Used by permission of Bethany House Publishers.

11

A. J. GORDON:
A God-Directed Man

Gordon College of Theology and Missions in Boston, Massachusetts, (now Gordon College and Gordon-Conwell Theological Seminary) was founded by the deeply devout Adoniram Judson Gordon. Originally he called it the Boston Missionary Training Institute, which indicates Gordon's intense interest in missions for which he was an advocate far and wide. He was also interested in prophecy, strongly upholding the personal, visible return of the Lord. He wrote on these and other subjects, including some incisive Bible studies and Christian life volumes, the *Schaff-Herzog* encyclopedia listing ten volumes he published, besides compiling two hymnbooks. He was also a collaborator with D. L. Moody.

A. J. Gordon boldly declared, "We evangelize or we fossilize," perhaps the first to popularize—if not originate—that phrase. Also attributed to Gordon is the statement, "One of the most fatal errors of the time is that ministers undertake to be feeders of men, instead of fishers of men" *(Hy Pickering in *One Thousand Acts and Facts).*

For the actual story of Gordon's taking Christ into his life, we are indebted to the biography, *Adoniram Judson Gordon*, by his son Ernest B. Gordon.

As has so often proven to be the case, a foundation laid by godly parents commonly bears fruit in their children coming to Christ. Of Gordon's own father we read: "Few men have left behind them such traditions of piety and devotion. The morning exercises of the family were held in a corner room of the old homestead, close to the crossroads, where the villagers were constantly passing. The recollection of Deacon Gordon's prayers . . . are still present in the minds of the older people. Rectitude, charity, self-denying effort for the advancement of the kingdom won the affection of the whole region. Strength and sweetness were here blended . . ."

And now of his mother we read: "A woman like Susannah Wesley, self-effacing in her unselfishness, quaintly unconscious of her own surpassing goodness, . . . unrecorded sacrifices for her twelve children. Her family was her parish; to them she ministered, and for them she ceased not to pray until the end."

As to A. J. Gordon's actual conversion his son writes, "The early years passed in a quiet village, in a home of exceptional piety, amid surroundings as could hardly fail to nurture a wholesome, high-souled character. When the boy reached his fifteenth year a great change passed across his inner life. Hitherto a thoughtless, somewhat indifferent, unresponsive lad, he now became intent on new things. A new seriousness sobered him; a new thoughtfulness was turning his attention to a larger life. . . . The weightier interests of the spiritual life began to absorb his thoughts.

"First came the struggle, the wrestling as at Peniel till the gray dawn. The conviction of sin was intense, unendurable. A realization of the corruption of the human heart, a vision of the perfect God, high and lifted up—to what conclusion could these lead save that of unqualified unworthiness, of utter helplessness? The conflict of soul darkened and intensified. A whole night was finally spent in such anguish of spirit that the father sat with him till daybreak. Sorrow endures for the night, but joy comes in the morning. Calm as the sunshine which flooded the hills the next day was that boy spirit which had found peace with God through our Lord Jesus Christ.

"On a lovely Sabbath in June he witnessed, with his two sisters, a good confession, going down with them in mystic death into the waters of the old mill-stream. His conversion was a new impulse in all directions. Books had been an aversion, study an almost penal discipline. With what avidity did he now go back to those distasteful tasks! For did they not constitute the anticipation and hope of which he was now treasuring in his heart? This hope and purpose he did not long keep to himself. Shortly after his sixteenth year had opened, he confessed before the church his determination to enter the ministry. . . . A shy, awkward boy, yet with light on his face, announcing, with much difficulty and stumbling, his purpose to devote his life and best powers to his Savior's work."

A. T. Pierson wrote: "His conversion was his turning toward Christ as his Savior and Lord. He believed the message that God gave his Son, that in Him is life everlasting. Instead of trying, he found peace in trusting, looking away to Jesus, as the Author and Perfecter of his faith."

And that was all that was needed to start one on a great career for his Master.

Pierson further wrote: "He was in every sense a great man; great in his mind and in his genius, having not only the administrative but the creative faculty; not only organizing but originating. His versatility was amazing." Then, speaking of Gordon's great Boston church, he says, "It was permitted to him, amid the atmosphere of Unitarianism and liberalism, to build up a believing brotherhood, characterized by as simple worship, pure doctrine, and primitive practice as any other in the world."

But Pierson is quick to add, "Let it not be thought that it cost Dr. Gordon nothing to renounce and resign the proud throne among pulpit orators and biblical scholars which his gifts seemed to offer, and seek simply to be a Spirit-filled man—consenting to be misunderstood, misrepresented, ridiculed, that he might be loyal to the still small voice within. . . . No review of his life, . . . must leave out his work as an author . . . these books constitute religious classics."

Dr. J. Christy Wilson, missionary to Iran for over twenty years, wrote: "Dwight L. Moody became aware of A. J. Gordon's effectiveness with students and invited him to serve as the main speaker at a student conference in Mount Hermon, Massachusetts. . . . Students were so moved by what they heard that, by the end of the conference 99 signed," indicating their purpose to be foreign missionaries. Further, "His church became a great mission-minded congregation. . . . At his death, his wife asked that flowers not be given but that money be donated for missions. One of the Chinese laundrymen who loved Dr. Gordon, put three one-dollar bills on his casket. This became part of a large missionary offering at his funeral. . . . His influence stretched around the world."

12

SIR WILFRED T. GRENFELL:
Missionary to Labrador

Sir Wilfred T. Grenfell, M.D., missionary to Labrador for 40 years and author of 24 books, outfitted the first hospital ship for North Sea fisheries and established hospitals and hospital ships throughout Labrador and off the coast of Greenland.

Among many of Dr. Grenfell's notable experiences was the occasion he set off with his dog team across a bay hoping to reach a need even though the ice was breaking up. But the weather suddenly changed, and he soon found himself hopelessly adrift on an ice pan heading for the open sea. His supplies, including cap and jacket, had all been lost in scrambling onto the ice pan. In that condition he realized that, as he was, he would soon die. He determined that there was but one way to keep alive. He selected three of his faithful and loyal dogs; then, one at a time with his back to the others, he killed them, using their skins to protect himself from the sub-zero cold. With leather thongs he joined their leg bones to make a staff, tied his much needed shirt to it and waved it in hopes of being seen. Though frostbitten, he survived until in the providence of God he was rescued.

The following is taken from a copy I have, autographed by him, of *What Christ Means to Me* (London: Hodder & Stoughten, 1926), written as he was steaming down, of all places, the Persian Gulf!

"As a boy, brought up in the orthodox teaching of the National

Church established by law in my native land [England], religion was a matter of course and part of every gentleman's education. It produced no more personal reaction that I was conscious of than in any other healthy lad. The only effect that I can remember was that I grudged having to 'waste' one day in seven, which, as we did not have to devote it to work, might of course have been used for games.

"Having a constitution hardy above the average, it never for a moment worried me as to what would happen if I died. I had no intention of dying, and so far as I could gather, religion seemed largely concerned with dying. At home we always had morning prayers—a custom which was tolerated rather than enjoyed. In the summer my parents generally went abroad to Switzerland or elsewhere, and then there were no morning prayers, and the day seemed freer and longer . . .

"I was not troubled by intellectual doubts. My next younger brother was very delicate, and I unusually devoted to him . . . But when he lay slowly dying, and I used to go every day to his room to bid him farewell, as I thought, everyone assured me that he would be absolutely all right once he died, and I was satisfied . . . I do remember being a bit surprised, however, that I was not more sorry when he died, surprised at my confidence in what everyone said, namely, that he had gone to a happier home somewhere else . . .

"When I was at public school, Christ as a person meant little to my consciousness. Our college proclaimed its faith in established religion as an institution . . . At fourteen years of age it was the right thing to be confirmed, after which you were allowed to stay to an after-service, when the younger boys had been dismissed. I distinctly remember, however, being a bit scared when, the first time I stayed to Communion, I heard the clergyman read out, 'He that partaketh unworthily, taketh it to his own damnation.' One always supposed that most of the masters accepted the college religion in its entirety. I am certain, however, that some did not. But that did not interest me at the time enough to raise a question in my mind as to where I stood . . ."

Later: "To keep my body fit and to excel in clean sport without neglecting my work or my patients was the larger part of any religion I possessed . . .

"One evening in 1883, going down a dark street on my way from a maternity case, I passed a great tent, something like a circus. A crowd had gathered, and I looked in to see what was going on. An aged man was praying on the platform before an immense audience. The length of the prayer bored me, and I started to leave as he droned on. At that moment a vivacious person near him jumped up and shouted: 'Let us sing a hymn while our brother finishes his prayer.' Unconventionality, common sense or humor in anything 'religious' was new to me. Brawling or disturbing the order or ritual is criminal in the established church.

"Someone said the interrupter was the speaker of the evening, so I stayed to hear him. I did not know anything about the man, nor did I see him again till fourteen years later, but he left a new idea in my mind . . . His illustrations were all from our own immediate environment, much as Christ's were, and the whole thing was so simple and human it touched everyone's heart . . .

"The preacher was an ordinary-looking layman, and I listened all the more keenly because I felt he had no professional axe to grind. Someone, after the meeting ended, gave me a booklet entitled *How to Read the Bible*, by D. L. Moody, the man to whom we had been listening, and during the next few days as I got time, I followed the advice in it and read the familiar legend with new interest and from a new viewpoint. I was searching for some guide to life in it, exactly as I sought in my medical textbooks a guide to physical treatment. I seemed to have suddenly waked up and to be viewing from outside the life which before I just took for granted as it came. The idea of this living *Leader* . . . Who could and did transform all who accepted Him, and Who in every rank of life everywhere literally would walk with ordinary folk and enable them 'to play the game' and 'endure as seeing Him who is invisible' fascinated me. It tallied also with all my knowledge of history and my personal experience . . .

"Some time later, I forget how long, some famous athletes, known to all the world interested in sports, were advertised to speak in East London—cricketers, oarsmen, athletes of national and international fame. I was intensely interested in hearing what they had to say. Seven of them, known on both sides of the Atlantic as the 'Cambridge Seven,' all went to China a little later. That their faith was no more an emotional flash in the pan than John's or Peter's or Paul's is proven by the fact that they are all still in the field thirty-five years later, though all are men of ample means to live at home in comfort. The speaker whom I actually heard was a great cricketer . . . After all these years I can still remember the whole drift of his talk. It was the old call of Joshua 'Choose today whom you will serve,' self, fear of comrades and others, or Christ.

"I felt then and I still believe today that he was absolutely right . . . I am so convinced that treading in the footsteps of the Christ explains the meaning of life, that even when I fail, not a shadow of doubt about it softens my sense of regret and self-condemnation . . .

"At the close of that address, the speaker urged all present who had made a decision to stand up. There were a number of my friends in the meeting, and I felt chained through fear to my seat. Sitting in the front semicircle of seats were almost a hundred husky lads, all dressed alike in sailor suits. They were from a training ship in the harbor. Suddenly one smallish boy got up and stood there, the target of many astonished eyes. I knew well what it would mean to him when the boys got back aboard, and it nerved me to stand up also. This step I have ever since been thankful for . . . Whatever else was the result of so apparently ephemeral a thing as a decision, it certainly entirely changed the meaning of life to me."

13

FRANCES RIDLEY HAVERGAL
God's Hymn Writer

The internationally known hymn writer, Frances Ridley
Havergal, was a well-educated poet who moved in the elite
circles of her day while always seeking to glorify her Lord.
Having learned to read when she was three, by the time she was
four she was reading the Bible. Soon she had memorized the four
Gospels, the Epistles, and Revelation, as well as Psalms, Isaiah, and
the Minor Prophets. At seven she was writing verses. Her mother
died when she was only eleven, and she was educated on the continent of Europe. She knew Latin, Greek, Hebrew, German,
French, Italian, and Welsh and read her Bible in the original Hebrew
and Greek. A highly cultured English lady, Miss Havergal was a fine
vocalist, could play the piano proficiently, and could have become
a concert artist.

Miss Havergal tells the story of her own conversion which
occurred apparently when she was about fourteen—after what
seemed quite a struggle for her in spite of having been familiar with
the Bible. Her account is taken from *Memorials of Frances Ridley
Havergal by her sister.*

"At times I utterly abominated being 'talked to,' and would do
anything on earth to escape kindly meant admonitions or prayers
offered for me.

"One spring I said to myself a dozen times a day, 'Oh, if God would but make me a Christian before the summer comes!' I could not think of another summer coming and going and leaving me still not a Christian. I shall know some day why my Father left me to walk thus alone in my childhood, why such long years of dissatisfaction and restlessness were appointed me, while others fancied me a happy, thoughtless child. But He must have been teaching me.

"I did so want to be happy, and to be a Christian. And I didn't at all see how I was to be, except by praying hard; and that I had done so often that I got quite disheartened at its resultlessness. At this time I don't think I had clear ideas about believing on the Lord Jesus, and so getting rid of the burden which had pressed so long upon my little soul. Now I was so uneasy that after nearly a fortnight's hesitation, I told my trouble to the Curate, saying especially that I thought I was getting worse, because I had not cared at all for Sunday afternoon reading or prayer. His advice did not satisfy me; so my lips were sealed to all but God for another five years or more.

"August, to my great delight, I went to Mrs. Tweed's school. She prayed that none might leave her roof unimpressed. Many dated from that time their real conversion to God. One after another, hitherto silent, spoke out and told what peace and joy in believing they had found, and blessed God that they ever came to that school. As I heard one and another speaking in such terms of confidence and gladness, my heart used to sink within me, it seemed so unattainable.

"Before long I had made a confidante of Miss Cooke (who afterward became her stepmother). She was visiting at Oakhampton at the same time with me, and had several conversations with me, each of which made me more earnest and hopeful. At last, one evening I sat on the drawing-room sofa alone with her, and told her again how I longed to know that I was forgiven.

"After more words she said, 'Why cannot you trust yourself to your Savior at once? Supposing that now, at this moment, Christ were to come in the clouds of heaven and take up His redeemed, could you not trust Him? Would not His call, His promise, be enough for you? Could you not commit your soul to Him, to your Savior, Jesus?' Then came a flash of hope across me which made me feel literally breathless. I remember how my heart beat. 'I could surely,' was my response; and I left her suddenly and ran away upstairs to think it out. I flung myself on my knees in my room, and strove to realize the sudden hope. I was very happy at last. I could commit my soul to Jesus. I did not and need not fear His coming. I could trust Him with my all for eternity. I could hardly believe it could be so, that I had really gained such a step. Then and there I committed my soul to the Savior; I do not mean to say without any trembling or fear, but I did—and earth and heaven seemed bright from that moment—I did trust the Lord Jesus."

Miss Havergal wrote several devotional books, including *Kept for the Master's Use* and *Royal Bounty*, as well as such well-known hymns as "I Gave My Life for Thee," "Who Is On the Lord's Side?" and "Like a River Glorious." She furnished the tunes for many of her own hymns. Perhaps her best-known hymn, "Take My Life and Let It Be," was translated into most European languages as well as several in Asia and Africa. The lines "Take my silver and my gold, Not a mite would I withhold," were no mere sentimental words with the author; the Lord put it upon her heart to take a precious jewel chest filled with valuable jewelry and send it all to a missionary society for furtherance of the gospel. As Kathleen Blanchard says, "The value of the legacy Frances Ridley Havergal left to humanity is beyond reckoning."

Frances corresponded across the Atlantic with the other Frances—Frances, or "Fanny," Crosby—even writing a poetic tribute to her. While the American Frances lived to be ninety-five, Miss Havergal died at the age of forty-two. For health reasons, her final days were spent in Swansea, South Wales. Duffield says, "She even learned Welsh from her donkey-girl to take part in the Welsh church services. . . . Her Christianity became her predominant characteristic, and her piety was as attractive as it was profound."

Reflecting on the ill health from which she suffered for years, she wrote in the "Prelude to F. R. H.'s Seventh Book, 1872" the following lines:

> "I would not shrink
> From suffering, if I may but sing for Thee. . . .
> As Thou has spared me to begin today
> The seventh small volume of these leaves of life,
> So let a sevenfold blessing rest upon
> All that will fill these pages."

14

MATTHEW HENRY:
The Commentator

As a small boy I can remember going with my father (in early days by horse and buggy) on wide ranging visits to pastors in scattered towns and villages. In their modest parsonages, the few books they could afford to possess were always a point of interest. And almost invariably among those treasured volumes would be found a set of *Matthew Henry's Commentary*. Not only would they be consulted in sermon preparation, but often Henry's pithy comments would be a subject for discussion, or, more to be cherished, some deep, heart-warming, soul-encouraging comment joyfully shared.

And not alone by preachers were these volumes prized, but also by Sunday school teachers, class leaders, devotional speakers, etc. Common people, too, would resort to these volumes frequently for simple spiritual encouragement and for daily reading in the family circle.

Although first published in the early 1700s, Matthew Henry's commentary has received wide-ranging commendations through the years, even to the present day. Warren Wiersbe recently wrote of it, "Probably the best-known commentary on the Bible in the English language . . . For a devotional and practical approach to Bible exposition, this commentary leads the way."[1]

When Wilbur M. Smith, in his widely consulted *Profitable Bible Study*, comes to list "Commentaries on the Entire Bible," we find only seven titles set forth, but when he comes to Henry's work he says, "Last of all, of course, a word about Matthew Henry's famous *Exposition of the Old and New Testaments*. In many ways he is the commentator of all commentators, and from his pages more ministers have derived material for sermons than from any other similar work published in our language . . . His commentary is distinctly devotional, and in this realm it will remain in the very first class as long as the Christian church is on earth."[2]

And Dr. Smith is not satisfied with references to Matthew Henry in but one of his volumes, but in his *Chats From A Minister's Library* he devotes a whole chapter to Henry, saying in part, "Everyone acknowledges that the greatest devotional commentary ever written in the English language, the work that undoubtedly has exercised more influence over ministers of the Gospel than any other one commentary, is the one written over two hundred years ago by Matthew Henry."[3]

The leading publisher of Matthew Henry in America, Fleming H. Revell Co., asked the late Dr. Charles G. Trumbull, long editor of the *Sunday School Times*, to write an introduction to a new edition. Trumbull says, "Matthew Henry digs deep down below the surface of God's Word; he sees truths hidden from most of us. He finds the most practical applications of God's wisdom to our everyday life; . . . Who can trace the streams of blessing that began to flow out from *Matthew Henry's Commentary* two hundred years ago?"[4] Trumbull finally refers to Amos R. Wells, "who owned a library of 24,000 volumes," and, incidentally, for many years edited Peloubet's annual Sunday school lesson volume, who said, speaking of the commentary, "that there was nothing else like it, that he used it all the time, and that he got a blessing from it each time he read it."

And surely we cannot overlook C. H. Spurgeon on this matter. In his famous *Commenting and Commentaries*, in which he cites over 1,400 titles, when he comes to "Commentaries on the Whole Bible," he lists 65 works. On Henry he says, "First among the mighty for general usefulness we are bound to mention the man whose name is a household word, Matthew Henry. He is most pious and pithy, sound and sensible, suggestive and sober, terse and trustworthy . . . He is usually plain, quaint, and full of pith . . . and from all deducing most practical and judicious lessons . . . suitable to everybody, instructive to all."[5]

Lest any think, as seems to have been implied, that Henry's work is of use principally because of its simplicity and appeal to very common people, it is of interest to observe that Augustus H. Strong, in his erudite *Systematic Theology*, quotes from it at least three times: on man's original state, on the nature of the atonement, and on the extent of the atonement.[6] And the scholarly James Orr, Editor of the *International Standard Bible Encyclopaedia*, in a lengthy article on commentaries, refers to its "genuine insight into the meaning of the sacred writer" (Henry knew Greek as well as Latin and French).[7]

But we must hasten on. It seems but natural, because of all said, to want to know something of how Henry came to know the Lord so fully. Indeed, one of his biographers, S. Palmer, "a contemporary," begins his *Memoirs* of Henry, saying, "Most readers of a work which has acquired such a degree of celebrity feel a desire to know something of the author; . . . Users of Henry's Commentary, which has long been in high repute in the religious world, will wish for some information concerning that excellent man."

The story begins with his father, the Rev. Philip Henry, a devout and faithful minister of the Nonconformists (or Dissenters). Born in 1662, Matthew "was so weakly as a child that no one expected him to live . . . He long continued weakly."[8] But, says another, "It is credibly stated that, at the early age of three years, he could read in the Bible with distinctness and observation . . . Extracts from a letter to his father when Matthew was only nine: 'Every day I have done my lesson of Latin, and two verses in the Greek Testament.'"[9] Daily morning and evening Bible reading in the home also surely lent their influence on the lad.

Matthew's father played a large part in the boy's conversion, his regular pulpit ministry furnishing a cumulative background. But finally one sermon in particular bore fruit. We read, Matthew's "first abiding convictions of religion, according to his own written account, were wrought when he was ten years of age in consequence of a sermon preached by his father on Psalm 51:17, 'The sacrifices of God are a broken spirit . . .' 'I think it was that,' says Matthew, 'that melted me; afterwards I began to enquire after Christ.'"[10]

Again we read, "For two or three days I was under great fear of hell . . . I having been engaged in serious examination—What hope I have that when I die I shall be received into heaven . . . If I never did this before, I do it now, for I take God in Christ to be mine. I give up myself to be his . . . Ministers have assured me that having repented of sin and believed on Christ, I am to believe that I am pardoned. I do really believe I am forgiven for Christ's sake. This is grounded on several scriptures . . ." The biographer quoting this then comments, "From this interesting document it is obvious that Mr. Henry, before he attained his eleventh year, was led into that vital and essential part of wisdom—the knowledge of the state of his own soul."[11]

Another biographer expresses it this way: "'Seek, and ye shall find,' is the promise. It was fulfilled to Matthew Henry, as it will be to all who plead it. He saw and believed in the atoning blood of Christ . . . Nor was this a cold, formal transaction. There had been 'grief, and shame, and sorrow for sin,' a believing on Christ for pardon, especially as pardoning his own sins . . ." This biographer, referring to the account that has come down to us, then says, "This record of early experience . . . is seen to be the record of a real event—the commencement of his true earthly and everlasting happiness."[12]

Somewhat similarly, but much, much later, Wilbur Smith gives us this regarding Henry's own account: "Recording his conversion, he writes, 'For spiritual mercies; for the Lord Jesus Christ . . ., for Grace, Pardon, Peace, . . . for Brokenness of Heart, for an Enlightening, Lord Jesus, I bless thee, . . . and I give thee thanks that I am and will be thine.' . . . In the same diary . . . he makes a statement concerning his love for the Word of God which we may call the spring from which all his later wonderful works on the Scriptures proceeded."[13]

Dr. Trumbull refers to additional labors of the one who gave us the commentary. "One marvels at the industry and devotion of the author who produced it, besides forty-five other books and pamphlets, in the midst of the many duties as pastor, preacher, and father, during a lifetime of fifty-two years."[14]

We may well conclude with an account of the difficulties of the times which gave us such a great man. In *A Popular History of the Free Churches,* Silvester Horne, says, "While Watts was laying the whole Church of Christ under lasting obligations by his revolutionising Church worship, another Nonconformist divine was quietly and laboriously completing a work of the highest value and significance. One of the ejected ministers was Philip Henry who suffered not a little for his Puritanism. It was immediately after his ejection that his son Matthew was born. The difficulty of exercising a Nonconformist ministry almost drove Matthew Henry to the law . . . Matthew Henry's commentary became the standard of exposition and held its supremacy for generations. He had a singularly full and fertile mind . . ."[15] We may be thankful that Matthew Henry did not continue with law (which he actually began). *God give us others today, willing to similarly pay the price to wholly follow Christ!*

---

1. Wiersbe, Warren W. *Victorious Christians You Should Know*, Grand Rapids, MI, Baker Book House, pp. 89, 93; 2. Smith, Wilbur M. *Profitable Bible Study*, p. 136; 3. Smith, Wilbur M. *Chats From A Minister's Library*, p. 159; 4. Trumbull, C. G. Matthew Henry's *Commentary*, Vol. I, opening page; 5. Spurgeon, C. H. *Commenting and Commentaries*, pp. 2,3; 6. Strong, A.H. *Systematic Theology*, 1907 edition; 7. Orr, James *International Standard Bible Encyclopedia*, Vol. II, p. 682; 8. Palmer, S. *Memoir*; 9. Williams, J. Bickerton, *Life of Henry*; 10. Palmer; 11. Williams; 12. Gordon, A. L., *Memoir*; 13. Smith, *Chats, op.cit.* pp. 160, 161; 14. Trumbull, *op.cit*; 15. Horne, C. Silvester; *A Popular History of the Free Churches*, pp. 251, 252.

Most biographical sketches are found in old editions of the commentary (if one is fortunate enough to come upon such).

15

H. A. IRONSIDE:
Ordained of the Lord

I first met Harry Ironside in 1922 when I was a young man. At that time Brother Ironside was active among the Plymouth Brethren and disdained being called "Dr. Ironside." Some years later, in Dallas, Texas, he took me out to lunch; and still later he asked me to speak to a group in the Moody Memorial Church which he pastored in Chicago, by which time he was nationally and internationally known.

Today Dr. Ironside is much appreciated through his widely-used Bible expositions and other writings. Although these works are simple and popular, they yet stand up against the most critical scholarship, of which Ironside had a very extensive knowledge through constant study.

The story of his conversion is taken from a pamphlet by him published many years ago, "My Conversion to God," although very much the same is found in E. Schuyler English's biography, *Ordained of the Lord* (Loizeaux Brothers, publisher).

"From a very early age God began to speak to me through His Word. I doubt if I could go back to the first time when, to my recollection, I felt something of the reality of eternal things. That I was lost and that Christ Jesus came from Heaven to save me were the first divine truths impressed on my young heart.

"To our home there often came servants of Christ—plain, godly men, who seemed to me to carry with them the atmosphere of eternity. Yet in a very real sense they were the bane of my boyhood. Their searching, 'Harry, lad, are you born again, yet?' or the equally impressive, 'Are you *certain* that your soul is saved?' often brought me to a standstill; I knew not how to reply.

"I had, it seemed to me, always believed, yet I dared not say I was saved. I know now that I had always believed *about* Jesus; I had not really believed in Him as *my* personal Savior. Between the two there is all the difference that there is between being saved and lost. A certain religiousness became, I suppose, characteristic. But religion is not salvation.

"I was nearly fourteen years old when, upon returning one day from school, I learned that a servant of Christ, well-known to me, had arrived. I knew before I saw him how he would greet me for I remembered him well and his searching questions when I was younger. Therefore I was not surprised, but embarrassed nevertheless, when he exclaimed, 'Well, Harry, lad, I'm glad to see you. And are you born again yet?' The blood mantled my face; I hung my head and could find no words to reply.

"'You don't know!' he exclaimed. 'Go and get your Bible, Harry.'

"I was glad to get out of the room, so went at once for my Bible and remained out as long as seemed decent, hoping thereby to recover myself. Upon re-entering the room, he said kindly, but seriously, 'Will you turn to Romans 3:19 and read it aloud?'

"Slowly I read, ' . . . that every mouth may be stopped, and all the world may become guilty before God.' I felt the application and was at a loss for words. The evangelist went on to tell me that he too had once been a religious sinner, till God gave him a sight of Christ. He impressed on me the importance of getting to the same place . . .

"Now Satan, who was seeking my soul's destruction, suggested to me, 'If lost, why not enjoy all the world has to offer so far as you are able to avail yourself of it?' I listened only too eagerly to his words, and for the next six months or thereabouts no one was more anxious for folly than I, though always with a smarting conscience.

"At last, on an evening in 1890, God spoke to me in tremendous power while out at a party with a lot of other young people, mostly older than myself, intent only on an evening's amusement. I remember now that I had withdrawn from the parlor for a few moments to obtain a cooling drink in the next room. Standing alone by the refreshment table, there came home to my inmost soul, in startling clearness, some verses of Scripture I had learned months before. I saw as never before my dreadful guilt in having so long refused to trust Christ for myself and in having preferred my own wilful way to that of Him who had died for me.

"I went back to the parlor and tried to join with the rest in their empty follies. But all seemed utterly hollow, and the tinsel was gone. The light of eternity was shining into the room, and I wondered how any could laugh with God's judgment hanging over us. We seemed like people sporting with closed eyes on the edge of a precipice, and I the most careless of all.

"That night I hurried home and crept upstairs to my room. There, after lighting the lamp, I took my Bible and, with it before me, fell upon my knees. I had an undefined feeling that I had better pray. But the thought came, 'What shall I pray for?' Clearly came back the answer, 'For what God has been offering me for years.'

"My dear mother had often said, 'The place to begin with is Romans 3 or John 3.' To these Scriptures I turned and read them carefully. Clearly I saw that I was a helpless sinner but that for me Christ had died and that salvation was offered freely to all who trusted Him. Reading John 3:16 the second time, I said, 'That will do. O God, I thank Thee that Thou hast loved me and given Thy Son for me. I trust Him now as my Savior, and I rest on Thy Word which tells me I have everlasting life.'

"Then I expected to feel a thrill of joy. It did not come. I wondered if I could be mistaken. I expected a sudden rush of love for Christ. It did not come either. I feared I could not be really saved with so little emotion. I read the words again. There could be no mistake. God loved the world of which I formed a part. God gave His Son to save all believers. I believed in Him as my Savior. Therefore I must have everlasting life. Again I thanked Him and rose from my knees to begin the walk of faith. God could not lie. I knew I must be saved."

Taken from the book, *Ordained of the Lord* by Schuyler English. Copyright © Loizeauz Brothers, Inc. Used by permission of Loizeaux Brothers, Inc.

16

ROBERT T. KETCHAM:
Foe of Compromise

Dr. Robert Thomas Ketcham was one of the great preachers of America through the large middle portion of this century. I was once told that so great was the esteem for him by Dr. Louis T. Talbot, pastor of the influential Church of the Open Door in Los Angeles, that he said that any time Dr. Ketcham was available he would be ready to turn over the pulpit of his church to Ketcham. More than once I have seen audiences—and I was among them—fall under the spell of Dr. Ketcham's fervent appeals.

But Ketcham made his mark by more than pulpit power. He will long be remembered as the implacable foe of modernism and compromise, exposing errors through pulpit and pen. He led the way in the formation of the General Association of Regular Baptist Churches. He edited its journal, *The Baptist Bulletin*, for many years. He wrote a number of books and numerous pamphlets. His *I Shall Not Want*, published by Moody Press, has gone through many printings (my copy lists seven printings through three years). Dr. Ketcham's deep interest and discernment has been so recognized as to merit his being placed on the board of several schools and mission agencies. He was even called as an expert to bear testimony in religious court cases (involving denominational issues). All this in spite of his being nearly blind in later years.

On a number of occasions I met and had personal fellowship with Dr. Ketcham. There were always many crowding around him, so I was highly privileged one time, after he had spoken at a special conference in the auditorium of the Church of the Open Door in Los Angeles, to drive him from that city to Long Beach. With only the two of us in the car, it was a rare opportunity for fellowship, as well as to drink in some of his rich wisdom.

Much more could be said of Dr. Robert T. Ketcham. But let us turn to the story of how he came into a personal relationship with Christ. The story of Bob Ketcham's conversion is taken from his biography, *Portrait of Obedience,* by J.M. Murdoch (Regular Baptist Press):

"In spite of the testimony of his mother and father, Robert entered his teens without claiming Christ as his personal Savior. He knew the Lord Jesus had died for his sins. He knew salvation came only through Christ. The positive influence of his parents' testimony was such that he knew Christ had performed the miracle of salvation in their lives. But his heart was hardened, and all his head knowledge was to no avail as he steadfastly refused to yield his life to Christ . . .

"As time passed, the discipline of a Christian home as exercised by godly parents was not acceptable to young Robert. At the age of sixteen he served notice on his father that he was [leaving home]. Charles Ketcham [his father], his heart aching with love, followed his son out of the rugged farmhouse . . . As the boy marched stiff-legged out the gate, his father called after him, 'Son, if you ever bump up against a row of stumps you can't pull, just call on Dad.' . . . As young Robert walked away from his home, his father poured out his heart to God: 'Lord, there goes my youngest son. You follow him and bring him back. I can't.' . . .

"Little did he know the emergencies that lurked before him, but he began to learn the truth in a hurry as he encountered stump after stump that he could not budge. Usually these were 'stumps' of his own sinful making; and usually he had to have his father come and pull him out of the tangled messes into which he had wandered. But still the stubborn lad refused to recognize the God of his earthly father as the answer to the needs of his heart.

"Finally the Spirit of God penetrated the hardened heart of young Bob Ketcham. On February 16, 1910, the twenty-year-old Allegheny mountain lad yielded to the Spirit of God and claimed the

Lord Jesus Christ as his personal Savior. His conversion took place in the Galeton Baptist Church. Gradually things began to change, but the first year of Ketcham's Christian life was anything but a roaring success. He tried to hang on to all of his old habits, and that simply did not work. He often described those early months of his Christian experience: 'I tried the experiment of hanging on to my cigarettes and my pool playing and my tenor singing and fooling around with the young people in the Galeton Baptist Church on Sundays. I got nothing out of this but a spiritual stomachache, and everybody around me got a spiritual headache.' . . .

"The young convert was not very fond of preachers, regarding them all as 'sort of stuffed shirts.' The only preacher Bob had any love for or confidence in was Harry S. Tillis, the pastor who preached the night he was saved. He liked Harry Tillis, and he liked the two-fisted approach Tillis used in the pulpit."

But young Bob Ketcham had a long way to go and a lot to learn before the fullness of our position before God became a reality to him. An experience some time after his acceptance of Christ illustrates both the boldness of the young man and his dire need of maturing in the things of Christ.

There came to his local church for a Bible conference a Bible teacher, W. W. Rugh. He taught by use of a large Bible chart which stretched across the front of the church. This intrigued the young man. "Bob was so fascinated by the messages on Sunday that he decided to go back to church on Monday night instead of going to the pool hall. Again he enjoyed the unique ministry of W. W. Rugh. Consequently, he forsook the pool hall on Tuesday evening and returned to church for an unprecedented third night in a row!"

The deep truth of our position in Christ was so new and unheard of to the young man that he was actually shocked. He thought that the pastor or some of the deacons (including his father) would challenge the speaker. Since none did, he broke right into the middle of the address: "Bob decided that it was his responsibility to do something about it. He stood to his feet and shouted, 'Mr. Rugh, I don't believe that!'"

The congregation was astounded, but the speaker was very patient with the young man and began to question him. When he was asked to turn to a passage in the seventeenth chapter of the gospel of John, it was revealed that Bob did not have a Bible. Mr

Rugh handed him his. "Robert took the Bible and started to search for John. He knew John was in there somewhere, but he had no idea where, so he kept searching. While he searched, Brother Rugh just stood there smiling and let him stew. Finally Bob found a John way at the back of the Bible near Revelation, but it did not have seventeen chapters. When he informed Rugh of this fact, the congregation snickered . . ." Bob had to be informed that there was a Gospel of John as well as an Epistle. When he was shown the verse of Scripture in question and asked to read it, Bob was more than dumbfounded, he was deeply convicted of the truth. "The scales of confusion fell, and Robert understood the miracle God performed when an individual accepted Christ as personal Savior.

"That night the whole Galeton church got a new look at what God does when He saves a person. And for the young man who had challenged the old preacher, the new understanding of the miracle of Salvation was to be used by the Spirit of God to work a permanent transformation. Old habits began to fall by the wayside . . ."

Only the years could tell the full story. After more than fifty years of eminent ministry behind him, Dr. Ketcham wrote to his own brother (also a minister): "The fact that God saved either one or both of us is still a marvel in the minds of the old residents of Galeton; and it is a marvel in our own eyes. We sure were a couple of unadulterated messes . . . Yes, the days of companionship in sin were by a miracle of God's grace changed into days of fellowship in the gospel ministry . . ."

Taken from the book, *Portrait of Obedience* by J. M. Murdoch. Copyright © Regular Baptist Press. Used by permission of Regular Baptist Press.

17

R. G. LeTourneau:
God's Businessman

Mr. R .G. LeTourneau was a genius in designing new and better earth-moving equipment. He established a number of manufacturing plants to satisfy worldwide demands but gave most of the profits to Christian enterprises. He was a leader in the Christian Businessmen's Organization and frequently spoke in churches, conventions, and other gatherings. He put the Lord first in his business—not a secular business with him when it was so fully dedicated to God.

It was my privilege to speak one weekend in R. G. LeTourneau's largest earth-moving plant then in Peoria. Arrangements were made for me to address the employees on a late-night-shift break. Having been taken to the factory well before the hour for speaking, I was escorted into Mr. LeTourneau's office. There I was directed to his chair behind a not-insignificant desk. I hesitated but was assured that Mr. LeTourneau was out of the city, and there was no problem at all. So I settled down in that imposing position, spreading some notes out on the desk in front of me. I had been thus occupied not long when the door burst open, and in marched "R. G." himself. In an apologetic manner I hastily began to gather my papers together and get up, but Mr. LeTourneau insisted upon my keeping my seat, saying, as he turned to his large drawing board a few feet away, that he wanted to work on some designs. I felt like a usurper and was relieved when I was finally summoned to the scheduled meeting.

The story of Mr. LeTourneau, including his conversion, is told in *God Runs My Business,* by A. W. Lorimer (Fleming H. Revell Co., 1941).

Mr. LeTourneau's personal salvation experience occurred when the family lived in Portland, Oregon. Young Robert quit school and went to work in a foundry. We read: "The heavy physical work of the foundry exactly suited his lively and restless nature. He had served about half of this time as an apprentice when he had the experience which changed the whole course of his life. This young man, strong of body, powerful of will, impatient of restraint, ambitious, imaginative and talented beyond his years, came suddenly to the Valley of Decision.

"He said of himself at this time: 'I was raised in a Christian home by my father and mother who loved Jesus and served Him with all their hearts. We had a family altar where we worshiped God. Father prayed and asked God to make his children useful in His kingdom. In spite of that, at the age of sixteen I found myself on the wrong road going the wrong way. I knew the right way, but I'd forget about it.'"

He continues his own story: "'About the time I was sixteen, I began to realize that something was wrong in my life. I tried to turn over a new leaf many times, but each time I failed and each time I got worse. It wasn't that I didn't know the Bible or the way of salvation. The trouble was I knew it too well. In our home we had to memorize Scripture, and I had memorized a great deal. But I recited it in a parrot-like way. I knew the words, but they had no meaning for me. Revival meetings would come to town, and I would go and get all worked up; but after the revival I'd go back to my old kind of life.

"'Then a special revival came and everybody said, "Are you going tonight?" and I said, "Oh, yes, I guess so." I went for four nights and then decided I wasn't getting anywhere. I was looking for something, but I didn't know exactly what. I thought I was seeking after God, but I was really seeking after the things which He had. The next night I stayed home and thought the whole thing over. I saw myself going down into sin and realized I was a lost sinner. The next night I went to the meeting, and when the altar-call was made,

I went forward. The workers asked me, "Do you believe that Christ died for sinners?" But I knew all the Scripture answers. There was something between my soul and salvation. I couldn't seem to get it; it wasn't real to me. I went home from that meeting that night and went to bed, and as I lay there, this thought came to me: If I should die tonight, I would go out into a lost eternity. Hell would be worse for me than for anyone else because I had heard the gospel and rejected it.

"'Then I cried out in desperation to God, "Lord, save me or I perish." Right there something happened. The glory of the Lord broke over me, and the full reality of salvation came into my soul.

"'My first thought was of my mother, who had been praying for my salvation for a long time. I thought she might be praying for me at that moment. I got out of bed and ran to her bedroom. "Mother," I said, "it's all settled now. You don't need to pray for me anymore; I am saved and on my way to heaven."' His mother wept tears for joy. This was the answer to her prayers."

LeTourneau himself comments, "How glad I am that we have a know-so salvation. Since that night I have never doubted that my sins were washed away."

The biographer concludes, "To see this self-confident youth, accustomed to conquering everything in his path, now conquered by the love of Christ was indeed a miracle of grace to those who beheld it."

———————

Taken from the book, *God Runs My Business: The Story of R. G. LeTourneau* by A. W. Lorimer. Copyright Fleming H. Revell Co. Used by permission of Fleming H. Revell Co.

18

DAVID LIVINGSTONE:
Explorer and Missionary

S o well known is the name of David Livingstone that it seems superfluous to try to introduce him. Acclaimed in his and succeeding days by the world at large as well as by a religious world of diverse persuasions as doctor and healer of untold suffering, explorer and geographer, scientist and classifier of biological and botanical specimens, missionary extraordinary, humanitarian and implacable foe of the slave trade, diplomat and pacifier of warring tribes, author and lecturer before the intelligentsia, he was above all, a sincere and humble Christian believer.

In London, our guide directed us around Westminster Abbey, pointing out the tombs of the great and famous—the most highly esteemed of the glory of the British empire. Here were the graves of 13 kings and 5 reigning queens (including Elizabeth I); over here, their great statesmen like William Pitt and Gladstone; there, poets from Chaucer, Spencer and Dryden to Browning, Tennyson and others. When he had finished and we were being escorted toward the door, I held back saying, "Just a moment; I want to see the tomb of David Livingstone."

Afforded a burial in the limited space among the world's renowned? Yes indeed, even though his heart had been removed and fittingly left in the heart of Africa. The whole world knew of his close walk with God when, after long being alone and weakened in body, he finally was found dead—kneeling by his cot in a position of prayer. *What a testimony!*

As a boy, David had the surpassing advantage of being raised in a godly home. He was also blessed in having a faithful Sunday school teacher. It is recorded that "at the age of nine he received a New Testament from his Sabbath School teacher for repeating the 119th Psalm on two successive evenings, with only five errors [176 verses]." But his new birth did not come easily. We read that "his tastes brought him into somewhat sharp collision with his Puritan father. His own decided preference was for books of travel and scientific works, and he had a strong aversion to the solid doctrinal and Calvinistic literature which his father tried to thrust on his attention."

The story of his actual conversion is recorded by W.G. Blaikie, his chief biographer, who in part quotes Livingstone's own words. "'Great pains had been taken by my parents to instill the doctrines of Christianity into my mind, and I had no difficulty in understanding the theory of a free salvation by the atonement of our Savior; but it was only about this time that I began to feel the necessity and value of a personal application of the provision of that atonement to my own case.' Some light is thrown on this brief account in a paper submitted by him to the directors of the London Missionary Society, in answer to a schedule of queries sent down by them when he offered himself as a missionary for their service. He says that about his twelfth year he began to reflect on his state as a sinner, and became anxious to realize the state of mind that flows from the reception of truth into the heart. He was deterred, however, from receiving the free offer of mercy in the gospel, by a sense of unworthiness to receive so great a blessing . . . Still his heart was not at rest; an unappeased hunger remained, which no other pursuit could satisfy.

"In these circumstances he fell in with Dick's *Philosophy of a Future State*. The book corrected his error, and showed him the truth. 'I saw the duty and inestimable privilege *immediately* to accept salvation by Christ. Humbly believing that through sovereign mercy and grace I have been enabled so to do, and having felt in some measure its effects on my still depraved and deceitful heart, it is my desire to show my attachment to the cause of Him who died for me by devoting my life to His service.'

"There can be no doubt that David Livingstone's heart was very thoroughly penetrated by the new life that now flowed into it. He did not merely apprehend the truth—the truth laid hold of him. The divine blessing flowed into him, subduing all earthly desires and wishes. What he says in his book about the freeness of God's grace drawing forth feelings of affectionate love to Him who bought him with His blood, and the sense of deep obligation to Him for His mercy, that had influenced his conduct ever since, is from him most significant. Accustomed to suppress all spiritual emotion in his public writings, he would not have used these words if they had not been very real. They give us the secret of his life" (Blaikie, pp. 29,30).

Having undergone a real conversion experience himself, Livingstone held strong convictions regarding the absolute priority of a genuine conversion experience for all. He himself said, "Nothing will induce me to form an impure church. Fifty added to the church sounds fine at home, but if only five of these are genuine, what will it profit in the Great Day? I have felt more than ever lately that the great object of our exertions ought to be conversions" (Quoted in Blaikie, p. 103).

His biographer further states, "He had very strong views of the spirituality of the Church of Christ, and the need of a profound spiritual change as the only true basis of Christian character." And Blaikie brings out that he maintained "civilization apart from conversion would be but a poor recompense for [the missionaries'] labor" (Blaikie, pp. 40,97).

These are convictions that need much to be pondered and heeded today!

19

MARTIN LUTHER:
Firebrand of the Reformation

If you visit the city of Rome, make it a point to "take in" the Church of the *Sancta Scala*—the church of the holy staircase. It may well be the site where there occurred one of the most momentous events in church history—the light that burst upon the soul of Martin Luther and turned his life into liberating channels.

Some who have surveyed the life of Luther feel that his conversion was a gradual process—a step-by-step realization of the truth. Others have pinpointed it—or at least identified the most crucial of the steps—as the time in 1511 when the young monk was on a pilgrimage to Rome.

Within the church referred to, an unusual sight may be seen: "pilgrims . . . climbing on their knees the Holy Stairs, where Luther received the gleam that started the Reformation" (William T. Ellis, *Bible Lands Today,* p. 16). D.E. Lorenz describes it: "This famous staircase, according to tradition, is the one which was in the house of Pilate, upon which Christ trod at the beginning of His way along the *Via Dolorosa*. Its casings have been repeatedly worn out by the knees of ascending pilgrims. This is the staircase that Luther was ascending on his knees when suddenly, with the battle-cry, 'the just shall live by faith,' he arose and walked away" (*The New Mediterranean Traveller,* p. 333).

A fuller description and account of Luther's experience is found in a leaflet by J.W.H. Nichols, published some years ago:

"There is in Rome an old building, quite unpretentious in appearance, but containing what is considered one of the most prized possessions of the Roman Catholic Church.

"Inside there is a flight of marble steps, in number twenty-eight. Tradition claims these to have been brought to Rome from Jerusalem, from the house of Pilate, who delivered the Lord Jesus Christ to be crucified. The steps are called *Sancta Scala* (holy stairs), and multitudes may be seen ascending them—young and old, rich and poor, moving up very slowly, for it is a painful process, seeing that they must ascend on hands and knees, to obtain meritorious (?) results. On every step the penitent offers a prayer, and they are told that if the full ascent is made in this way, they may eventually obtain absolution at some future time, but when and where seems uncertain.

"About four centuries ago, a young Saxon monk travelled to Rome, lashed by a tormenting conscience and heavily burdened with a load of sin. In his zeal he had come to make the ascent, hoping thus to be rid of his burden and obtain the favor of God. He joined the company on the marble steps and conscientiously began the ascent on hands and knees, repeating his prayers. He had laboriously reached halfway, when suddenly he heard a voice proclaiming in his inmost soul: *'The just shall live by faith.'* Twice before these same words had reached his consciousness, but they were crowded out by a man-made theology. Now memory is stirred, and the precious message of the grace of God reached the heart of Martin Luther upon the 'holy stairs,' and the burden of unforgiven sin was rolled away. Luther became a new creature in Christ Jesus, the shackles of Romish superstition were cast away, and henceforth he rejoiced in preaching the forgiveness of sins and justification through faith alone.

"Back to Germany he returned, and from that time proclaimed in no uncertain words that blessed and soul-emancipating truth of *justification by faith* to the joy and blessing of thousands."

Professor Kostlin, in one of the most authentic lives of Luther (translated from the German), describes something of the workings of Luther's mind relating to this incident, some of the highlights of which are:

"The devotion of a pilgrim inspired him as he arrived at the city which he had long regarded with holy veneration. It had been his wish, during his troubles and heart-searchings, to make one day a regular and general confession in that city. When he came in sight of her, he fell upon the earth, raised his hands and exclaimed, 'Hail to thee, holy Rome!' . . . He declared afterwards how he had run like a crazy saint on a pilgrimage through all the churches and catacombs and had believed what turned out to be a mass of lies and impostures. He was shocked by all that he observed of the moral and religious life and doings at this center of Christianity . . .

"In all this he found no real peace of mind; on the contrary, his soul was stirred to the consciousness of another way of salvation which had already begun to dawn upon him. While climbing on his knees and in prayer the sacred stairs which were said to have led to the judgment hall of Pilate and where, to this day, worshipers are invited by the promise of Papal absolutions, he thought of the words of St. Paul in his epistle to the Romans (1:17), 'The just shall live by faith.'"

The Word of God had its impact; may it ever be so!

20

F. B. MEYER:
Pastor to the World

One time I was asked by a group of eager young ministers to recommend a few of the old-time stalwarts in the faith, some leading Bible teachers whose works were thoroughly sound, sane and spiritual, and those which might prove helpful to them. At the top of the list I believe I named F. B. Meyer and A. T. Pierson.

I have two biographies of Meyer. The one written after his death (1929) by his close friend, W. Y. Fullerton, acknowledges that the earlier one, by M. Jennie Street, gives in more chronological order the events of his life. Both will richly reward the reader, but we take the story of his early life and conversion chiefly from the one by Street, a beautifully written account.

First, however, we may note some salient features of Meyer's extraordinary career. Since his helpful writings have been alluded to, they may here be noted. After speaking of other influences of his life, Fullerton says, "Perhaps the most evident legacy is the books he wrote, more than seventy of them in English, many translated into other languages (twenty in Swedish alone) and pamphlets enough to complete the hundred."

Jennie Street, writing more than twenty-five years before his death, reports of his books, "In America they are almost as well known as in England, and it is stated on good authority that in Australia there is scarcely a house which does not possess some of them. They have been translated into many tongues; every volume into German . . . Most of his books have been rendered into Swedish, and the good Queen of Sweden is among their most appreciative readers. Several works have been done into Hindi, Singalese, Burmese, Chinese, modern Greek, and other languages . . . The first result of the translation of one book into Syrian was the conversion of the translator!"

Fullerton's accounting of his writings at the time of his death is: Bible biographies (character studies), twelve; the Daily Homily, five, plus eight other devotional books; books on spiritual living, twelve; expository works, nine; sermons, eight volumes; solid essays (like *Where are our Dead,* and *Expository Preaching*), fourteen volumes. Then Fullerton adds, "He also wrote at least thirty-five booklets which have had a phenomenal circulation, exceeding two millions."

While, as Fullerton says, "During his life edited several magazines," he did not limit his efforts to literary work. The *Wycliffe Biographical Dictionary of the Church* reports, "he engaged in social, temperance, and reclamation work. Became a politician and Borough Councilor; headed a movement to close saloons; was the means of shutting up nearly five hundred immoral houses; labored for the reclamation of released prisoners; and effected organizations for all ages and classes . . . Conducted missions in South Africa and the far East . . . the United States, Canada, Jamaica, Australia, and the Near East." And Street tells how "he had an interview with President McKinley at the White House."

When the then unknown D. L. Moody came to England, Meyer sparked the encouragement and support needed to establish Moody. Then he, along with A. T. Pierson, became close associates of Moody, and together they built up the well-known Bible conference centers in America.

But we must get to the story of Meyer's conversion. As extracted from Street:

"Prayed for and prayed with and watched over from the beginning, Freddy Meyer was surrounded with the holiest influences, and from his earliest childhood he responded to them. At four years of age his parents traced with joy the unmistakable signs of that grace which enables those who are old in years and sin to become as little children, and which is never lovelier than when it is displayed in a child's heart and life. Before he was five years old he loved prayer and delighted in having the Bible read to him. He was fond of learning hymns and early showed great aptitude for quoting them appropriately.

"His childish prayers were generally made in his own words and were most evidently the expression of his wishes. Soon after his sixth birthday he told his mother that he was quite sure God had forgiven his sins; and the affectionate eyes that watched him noted that he was eager 'to be good,' thoughtful if anyone was in trouble, and deeply penitent for childish faults. Very often his mother heard that he had been saying hymns in bed, and a nurse noticed that he sometimes found opportunities to pray alone. Of his own accord, after one of his mother's lessons, he added to his evening prayer the petition, 'Put Thy Holy Spirit in me.' Once he asked with a puzzled look, 'What do people mean by being afraid to die? Why are they? I am not.'

"After breakfast on Sunday mornings, the mother gathered the children about her to read the Bible to them. As they grew older they had passages to commit to memory, and references to find. So, under his mother's guidance, the future preacher laid the foundation of that wide and accurate knowledge of the Book of books which makes his sermons and addresses so rich in Scriptural quotations and allusions. At half-past four on Sundays the children felt that the climax of the day had come, for then their mother played hymns on the piano, and their father's fine bass voice led the children's singing.

"As Freddy grew older, he was encouraged to read his written notes of the morning sermon. When he was nine years old he gave his mother a paper on which was written: 'This is for my dear parents, and I hope they will be pleased with it, for I am going to be a minister if God lets me live so long. And now I am happy, for I think God has given me a new heart.'"

A few final comments. This from Street: "An American minister who first met him at Northfield has given this description. 'With beautiful frankness he tells of his own secret struggles and failings, so that no one would put him on an unapproachable pedestal . . . He believes in present freedom from known sin and in endless progress in fulness of blessing.'"

Another friend speaks of "his enormous capacity for work and the constancy of his walk with God . . . When opportunity serves, he never misses a chance of personal evangelism. Once he was grateful for a secretary's mistake which entailed a drive in an open vehicle on a wet and windy day, because it gave him time for two special talks, first with a news agent, and then with the driver of the carriage."

Hy Pickering is responsible for this: "Meyer is said to have preached 15,000 sermons. In his eightieth year he addressed 300 meetings, and celebrated his 81st birthday by preaching morning and evening."

A. L. Glegg said: "He was a pilgrim down here, his real home was in Heaven."

21

DWIGHT L. MOODY:
Shoe Store Conversion

The name of D. L. Moody is so universally recognized that little need be said to remind us who this notable man was. Moody was acknowledged on every hand as having been modern history's most outstanding evangelist. This high regard remains undiminished.

Remembered chiefly as an evangelist, Moody, who had no formal training for the ministry and was never ordained, founded a great church, three schools—the best known one in Chicago—summer conference centers and a publishing agency. He made several preaching tours of the British Isles, on one holding forth in London alone for five months. It is estimated that "he traveled more than a million miles" *(New International Dictionary of the Christian Church)*, and that, before the days of air travel.

One source suggests "Moody's success as an evangelistic preacher was the fruit of his undaunted courage in spite of all opposition, the frankness, vigor, and urgency of his appeal . . ." *(The Oxford Dictionary of the Christian Church)*. Another declares, and this well before the day of radio, that his was "a life of great influence, popularity, and power . . . Hundreds of thousands, if not millions of people, became Christians" through his ministry *(Wycliffe Biographical Dictionary of the Church)*.

The first part of Moody's story we take from the account by his

93

son-in-law, A. P. Fitt. He says of young Moody, "he went to Boston where he had a homesick and trying time seeking work and finding none. At last he approached his uncles again and was probably in such a condition that they were able to make their own terms with him. They agreed to take him into their store if he would promise to attend church and Sabbath-school and not to drink or gamble.

"Dwight became the store boy to do odds and ends. His ambition now was to make one hundred thousand dollars and be a successful merchant. He made up for the deficiencies in polish and externals by a natural wit and brightness that lifted him out of his lowly position and brought him to the front as a salesman.

"His first definite spiritual experience came to him during his stay in Boston—his conversion.

"Attendance at church and Sabbath-school was obligatory under the agreement with his uncle. But it was merely formal at first. The earnest, cultured addresses of Dr. Kirk did not reach young Moody. It is said he chose a seat in one of the obscurest pews in the gallery, and that, wearied with the hard work of the week, he used to sleep most of the time during the Sunday services.

"In the Sabbath-school he was placed in a class taught by Edward Kimball. The teacher handed him a Bible and told him the lesson was in John. Moody took the book and hunted all through the Old Testament for John. The other young men (among whom were some Harvard students) detected his ignorance and nudged each other. The teacher saw his embarrassment and found the place for him. 'I put my thumb in the place and held on,' said Mr. Moody afterward. 'I would not be caught there again'—an incident that exhibits, not merely his ignorance of the Bible, but also his dogged purpose to learn from his mistakes."

Turning now to Will Moody's biography of his father, we get more of the details of Dwight's actual conversion. "Mr. Moody had never experienced the regenerating work of God's Spirit by a definite acceptance of Christ. In theory he knew that giving way to a violent temper was wrong, but in his self-will he found it hard to yield to restraint. But in Sunday-school his Bible-class teacher had been gradually leading the young man to a fuller knowledge of God's plan of salvation until it needed only an additional personal interview to bring him to that decision of the will which should determine whether he would accept or reject God's provision for overcoming sin and entering into harmony with Himself. The opportunity for this interview was not a chance event but one carefully and prayerfully sought by Mr. Kimball, who thus relates the story of Dwight L. Moody's conversion:

"'I was determined to speak to him about Christ and about his soul and started down to Holton's shoe store. When I was nearly there, I began to wonder whether I ought to go in just then during business hours. I thought that possibly my call might embarrass the boy and that when I went away the other clerks would ask who I was and taunt him with my efforts. In the meantime I had passed the store and, discovering this, I determined to make a dash for it and have it over at once. I found Moody in the back part of the building wrapping up shoes. I went up to him at once, and, putting my hand on his shoulder, I made what I afterwards felt was a very weak plea for Christ. I simply told him of Christ's love for him and the love Christ wanted in return. That was all there was. It seemed the young man was just ready for the light that then broke upon him, and there, in the back of that store in Boston, he gave himself and his life to Christ.'

"From the moment that Moody accepted Christ his whole life changed. Whereas church attendance had been observed simply because it was a duty, from this time forth for nearly fifty years he found his greatest joy in the service of God.

"'Before my conversion,' as he himself used to express it, 'I worked toward the Cross, but since then I have worked from the Cross; then I worked to be saved, now I work because I am saved.'

"Forty years afterward, preaching in Boston, he thus described the effects of his conversion upon his life:

"'I can almost throw a stone to the spot where I found God over forty years ago. I wish I could do something to lead some of you young men to that same God. He has been a million times better to me than I have been to Him.

"'I remember the morning on which I came out of my room after I had first trusted Christ. I thought the old sun shone a good deal brighter than it ever had before; as I heard the birds singing in the trees I thought they were all singing a song to me. Do you know, I fell in love with the birds. It seemed to me that I was in love with all creation. I had not a bitter feeling against any man, and I was ready to take all men to my heart. If a man has not the love of God shed abroad in his heart, he has never been regenerated.'

"After his conversion young Moody was no less energetic and ambitious in the interests of the Kingdom of God than he had been in business."

We conclude by returning for a few words to Mr. Fitt's account: "Mr. Moody was very solicitous in later years about persons being admitted to membership in our churches without really having been 'born again' and directed his efforts to bring men and women face to face with this question, to see not only if they had become partakers of the divine nature, but also that with Paul they should be able to say, 'I *know* whom I have believed.'

"Mr. Kimball wrote, 'I can truly say that I have seen few persons whose minds were spiritually darker when he came into my Sabbath-school class, or one who seemed more unlikely ever to become a Christian of clear, decided views of gospel truth, still less able to fill any sphere of extended public usefulness.' Dr. Kirk and the church officers lived to thank God for Mr. Moody's marvelous development in grace and in the knowledge and service of our Lord and Savior Jesus Christ."

22

G. CAMPBELL MORGAN:
Britain's Gifted Bible Teacher

So widely recognized is G. Campbell Morgan that the *Funk & Wagnalls New Standard Encyclopedia* reports on him. Later sources add much more. Wilbur M. Smith *(A Treasury of Books for Bible Study)* reports, "He was for some years president of Chestnut College, Cambridge University, he made many trips to America; he established a Bible Teachers Association; he edited *The Westminster Record* for four years, *The Westminster Pulpit* for eleven years, *The Westminster Bible Record* for eight years, and the *Mundsley Conference Report* for eight years . . . By 1930, a previous biographer tells us, he had published seventy-two volumes!" In another place, Mr. Smith speaks of his sermons as "the greatest Biblical preaching of the twentieth century." Mr. Smith also quotes James M. Gray who, in the *Moody Monthly* (1930), spoke of Morgan as "the most outstanding preacher that this country has heard during the past thirty years."

Having understood that G. Campbell Morgan was one of the greatest preachers of the day, I was desirous to hear him when he was to occupy the pulpit of one of the largest churches in southern California. I was young and I asked a neighbor, a brilliant retired physician, to accompany me. Neither of us—the simple minded younger nor the astute older one—was disappointed.

As I remember him, Dr. Morgan did not engage in highly dramatic oratory. Rather, calm, direct, but forceful delivery. What was most notable, however, for the careful listener, was the keen, logical analysis of his chosen Bible text; his clear, incisive, well-organized exposition; and his driving home points that might easily be overlooked by the casual reader.

And how did Campbell Morgan come into a knowledge of the Savior? We take the story from his biography, *A Man of the Word,* by his daughter-in-law, Jill Morgan. It goes back to the subject's early days. We read, "It was an era of great preaching . . . During the holidays the boy was taken by his father to hear many of those whose names, forgotten now, were then famous in religious circles. Some were Welshmen who came out of their native hills with all the fire and intensity of the Old Testament prophets. The doctrines of the faith were expounded. Sinners were challenged and brought face to face with judgment and redemption . . .

"An event of the greatest importance occurred in 1873, an event which moved England in her national as well as in her religious life, for it was in the summer of that year that Mr. D. L. Moody and his equally gifted companion, Mr. Ira D. Sankey, came on their preaching mission. 'I saw neither of them during that visit,' Dr. Morgan says, 'but like thousands of others, came as a boy under the influence of the ministry of song.' The vibration of their presence in any town ran through all the country. 'Those vibrations found their way into our home and into my life,' he continues . . . Mr. Moody's preaching had tremendous effect upon England, and a great religious revival swept the country . . . Whatever may be the influences of his environment, a small boy soaks them up like a sponge. This child [Morgan] had lived his few years in an atmosphere of preaching, and [in] an absence of almost all counter-attractions.

"Attendance at the services of the church, Biblical training in the home, and family worship took hours out of the week . . . The Victorian era made for high ideals and a precocity in some natures which blossomed into an early maturity. Time was to make of this youngster—this paradox of fun and gravity, so impressionable and yet so unyielding—a man after God's own heart, with a message pertinent for his generation . . .

"Until he was sixteen years of age, Dr. Morgan declared it had never entered his mind to doubt the authority of the Bible. At home and in school it was held in reverence as the only revelation of truth. 'I did not think,' he said, 'there could be any honest and respectable man who could doubt that the Bible was the Word of God. Then I found myself plunged into a world of which I had no knowledge up to that time . . . The whole intellectual world was under the mastery of physical scientists and a materialistic and rationalistic philosophy. I was as honest then as now, and gradually faith, while not undermined, was eclipsed. When the sun is eclipsed the light is not killed, it is hidden. There came a moment when I was sure of nothing.'

"This young man felt the troubled waters of the stream of religious controversy carrying him beyond his depth. He read the new books. He became confused and perplexed. No longer was he sure of that which his father proclaimed and had taught him in the home . . .

"The more he read, the more unanswerable became the questions which filled his mind. One who has never suffered it cannot appreciate the anguish of spirit young Campbell Morgan endured during this crucial period of his life. At last the crisis came when he admitted to himself his total lack of assurance that the Bible was the authorative Word of God to man."

He took all of his books and locked them up in a cupboard. The story goes on, "He went down the street to a bookshop. He bought a new Bible and, returning to his room with it, he said to himself: 'I am no longer sure that this is what my father claims it to be—the Word of God. But of this I am sure. If it be the Word of God, and if I come to it with an unprejudiced and open mind, it will bring assurance to my soul of itself. That Bible found me,' he said. 'I began to read it then; I have been a student of it ever since.'

"At the end, Campbell Morgan emerged from that eclipse of faith absolutely sure that the Bible was, in very deed and truth, none other than the Word of the living God. With this crisis behind him [there was a] new certainty thrilling his soul."

The impress of that yielded life lives on. One hundred years after his birth, a writer in *Christianity Today* (June 7, 1963), said, "Campbell Morgan was probably the most competent, certainly the most popular, Bible teacher of his time." But not only of his own time. *The Wycliffe Biographical Dictionary of the Church,* 1982, says his "work lives on today in a real way in his many writings . . .

Authored a large number of Bible commentaries, sermons, and other books on theology . . ."

We might have mentioned that it is no wonder that D. L. Moody, in later years, brought Morgan to his Northfield conferences and R. A. Torrey to his Montrose center, and others to equally noted places of ministry. But why go on? I have, I believe, in my library a score or more of Morgan's volumes, and they are still well regarded.

23

ANDREW MURRAY:
South African Pastor and Author

Today we think of Andrew Murray chiefly as a writer of many helpful books on vital aspects of the Christian life. Indeed, he produced numerous works which have gone through repeated printings and are still highly commended, having proved a great blessing through the years.

But a review of Mr. Murray's life (1828-1917) will bring out much more. He was greatly concerned with evangelism, engaging in many evangelistic preaching tours even to advanced years. Likewise, he was deeply burdened for missions, promoting and taking part in mission conferences. He rejoiced when more than one of his children volunteered for the mission field. One of his books, much discussed in its day, was *The Key to the Missionary Problem* (introductory words by H. C. G. Moule; my copy of many years is a fourth edition, American Tract Society, NY). Recently (1984) another reprint edition is employed as the basis of a missions course for credit. Long ago F. B. Meyer wrote of it, "If it were read universally throughout our churches by ministers and people alike, I believe it would lead to one of the greatest revivals of missionary enthusiasm that the world has ever known."

Mr. Murray was also much concerned about youth work, which he advocated and helped even to the late years of his life. The first edition of his well-known book, *The True Vine,* was dedicated to a then flourishing youth effort (the International Society of Christian Endeavor). He also established and directed schools, seminaries and, finally, training institutes for the underprivileged.

He was interested in the Keswick movement, was a leading participant, and later established a South Africa branch. On the urgent invitation of D. L. Moody, he spoke at conferences, like that at Northfield, Massachusetts, and lectured at the Moody Bible Institute.

Besides all this, Mr. Murray was much occupied as moderator of the largest denomination in South Africa, which long recognized his leadership and which he helped steer through many a crisis.

Showing his rounded-out character, the *Wycliffe Biographical Dictionary of the Church,* says, "Mr. Murray's time was in much demand among the churches of Cape Colony, Orange Free State, Transvaal, and Natal. At his insistence his Church consented to permit him to use half of his time in itinerant evangelism . . . Following Mrs. Murray's death, he devoted his last twelve years to conventions and evangelistic meetings in the United States, Canada, England, Ireland, Scotland, Holland, and South Africa."

Where, then, we may well wonder, did he find time to write? He carried on a voluminous correspondence. He wrote approximately 240 books and booklets published in fifteen languages! One biographer says his teachings "were translated with equal profit into French, German, Italian, Spanish, Swedish, Danish, Russian, Yiddish, Arabic, Armenian, Telugu, Malaysian, Japanese and Chinese"!

We take the story of Mr. Murray from the biography by W. M. Douglas, *Andrew Murray and His Message,* a book which has gone through a number of editions. Here we gather but the highlights.

Andrew Murray was raised in a godly home—his father was a minister—where the things of the Lord were constantly set before the children. When Andrew and his brother, studying in Scotland, were written to by their father to give serious thought to what career they might follow, they replied that they were inclined toward the ministry. The father replied that he was pleased, but very wisely added, "I trust, however, my dear boy, that you have given your heart to Jesus Christ, to be His now and forever, to follow Him through good and through bad report."

The boys went to Holland for advanced studies in the Dutch language. We read, "In Holland Andrew Murray entered into the assurance of salvation. He conveys this great news to his parents thus: 'My Dear Parents; It was with great pleasure that I today received yours of the 15th of August, containing the announcement of the birth of another brother. And equal, I am sure, will be your delight when I tell you that I can communicate to you *far gladder tidings, over which angels have rejoiced, that your son has been born again.* It would be difficult for me to express what I feel in writing to you on the subject . . .

"'When I look back to see how I have been brought to where I now am, I must acknowledge that, "He hath brought the blind by a way that he knew not, and led him by a path he had not known." . . . After leaving [Scotland], however, there was an interval of seriousness, during the three days at sea: our departure from Aberdeen—the voyage—the recollections of the past, were all calculated to lead one to reflect. But after I came to Holland I think I was led to pray in earnest, more I cannot tell, for I know it not, but "Whereas I was blind, now I see." I was long troubled . . . yet I trust and at present feel as if I could say, I am confident that as a sinner I have been led to cast myself on Christ. I call on you to praise the Lord with me. At present I am in a peaceful state; I think I enjoy a true confidence in God.'"

The biography continues, "On the eve of his 18th birthday he writes, 'Tomorrow will close a year which is certainly the most eventful in my life, a year in which I have been made to experience most abundantly that God is good to the soul that seeketh Him . . . I rather think when I last wrote I gave an account of what I believed was my conversion, and God be thanked, I still believe that it was His work.'"

Writing many years later he said, "My justification was clear as the noonday, I knew the hour in which I received from God the joy of pardon."

Later, Murray himself said, "Oh! how easy and content have I been living while souls have been perishing. How little have I felt the compassion with which Christ was moved when He wept over sinners. Love to souls so filling the heart that we cannot rest because of them would lead us to be very different from what we are."

The biographer reports, "Mr. Murray was always in great

request as an evangelist." And Murray himself said, "The more I travel the more I see that the great need of our church is Evangelists. It does almost appear wrong not to undertake the work when one knows that there are hundreds ready to be brought in. It appears terrible to let them go on in darkness and indecision . . . Oh! why should not our hearts be filled with the love which wrestles for souls."

We will conclude with the author's observation, "It will appear how wonderfully God used His servant as an Evangelist at an age when most men feel the work of their lives is finished. Very wonderful was the harvest God enabled His faithful old servant to gather."

24

JOHN NEWTON:
Slave Ship Captain Saved by Grace

The dramatic, life-transforming change wrought in John Newton has, down through the years, evoked both amazement at the contrast produced and widespread recognition of it as an outstanding example of the regenerating power of the gospel.

Who could have imagined that some of the world's best loved hymns, like *Amazing Grace! How Sweet the Sound,* could have been written by one who began in England the wild life of a seaman at the age of eleven (his mother having died), abandoning his ship was captured by a press-gang for service in a British naval vessel, deserted, recaptured, publicly flogged as a felon and degraded in rank, abandoned in Africa, given over to treatment as a slave among blacks, imprisoned, twice escaping death miraculously, followed by a life of "sad and wanton profligacy" and years of anti-religious sentiment and blasphemy; yet later could pen the widely sung *How Sweet the Name of Jesus Sounds.*

After his initial experience with God, Newton passed through years of spiritual struggle with little outward encouragement, but finally turned his life over to the ministry of the Word of God. He learned Greek, Hebrew, and Syriac; wrote several highly commended works, along with such well-known hymns as *Safely Through Another Week.* Indeed, Duffield's *English Hymns* lists 32 by Newton (and Duffield's standard work devotes over eight pages to the story of Newton).

Newton became a close friend of the poet William Cowper and with the latter's collaboration produced the famous *Olney Hymns*. Having once commanded a ship in the slave trade, Newton wrote vigorously against that nefarious traffic, even arousing William Wilberforce who then became the great British emancipator.

After years of a wicked and dissolute life, though frequently experiencing undeserved mercies from God, it was a storm at sea which at last aroused his conscience and to which he himself attributed the beginning of his changed state. We take the story from the account of Richard Cecil, revised by Newton himself (here presented with numerous details omitted).

"With the length of this voyage in hot climate, the vessel was greatly out of repair, and very unfit to support stormy weather; the sails and cordage were likewise very much worn, and many such circumstances concurred to render what followed more dangerous.

"My conscience witnessed against me once more, and I concluded that I must abide the consequences of my own choice. I put an abrupt end to these reflections by joining in with some vain conversation. But now the Lord's time was come, and the conviction I was so unwilling to receive was deeply impressed upon me by an awful dispensation.

"I went to bed that night in my usual security and indifference, but was awakened from a sound sleep by the force of a violent sea which broke on board us. So much of it came down below as filled the cabin I lay in with water. This alarm was followed by a cry from the deck that the ship was going down. It was filling with water very fast. The sea had torn away the upper timbers on one side and made the ship a mere wreck in a few minutes. Taking in all circumstances, it was astonishing and almost miraculous that any of us survived.

"We expended most of our clothes and bedding to stop the leaks (though the weather was exceedingly cold, especially for us who had so lately left a hot climate), over these we nailed pieces of boards. I pumped hard and endeavored to animate myself and my companions. I told one of them that in a few days this distress would serve us to talk of over a glass of wine, but he being a less hardened sinner than myself, replied with tears, 'No, it is too late now.'

"I was obliged to return to the pump, and there continued till noon, almost every passing wave breaking over my head, but we made ourselves fast with ropes that we might not be washed away. Indeed, I expected that every time the vessel descended in the sea, she would rise no more. And though I dreaded death now, and my heart foreboded the worst, if the Scriptures, which I had long since opposed, were true indeed, yet still I was but half convinced and remained for a space of time in a sullen frame, a mixture of despair and impatience. I thought if the Christian religion were true I could not be forgiven, and was therefore expecting, and almost at times wishing, to know the worst of it.

"The 10th of March is a day much to be remembered by me, and I have never suffered it to pass wholly unnoticed: on that day the Lord sent from on high and delivered me out of deep waters. I continued at the pump, and then I could do no more. I went and lay down upon my bed, uncertain and almost indifferent whether I should rise again. In an hour's time I was called, and not being able to pump, I went to the helm and steered the ship till midnight. I had here leisure and convenient opportunity for reflection. I began to think of my former religious professions, the extraordinary turns in my life, the calls, warnings and deliverances I had met with; the licentious course of my conversation, particularly my unparalleled effrontery in making the gospel history the constant subject of profane ridicule. I thought, allowing the Scripture premises, there never was nor could be such a sinner as myself; and then I concluded that my sins were too great to be forgiven. I waited with fear and impatience to receive my doom.

"When I heard in the evening that the ship was freed from water, there arose a gleam of hope; I thought I saw the hand of God displayed in our favor: I began to pray. I began to think of that Jesus that I had so often derided; I recollected his death: a death for sins not His own, but, as I remembered, for the sake of those who in their distress should put their trust in Him. The Lord was pleased to show me at that time, the absolute necessity of some expedient to interpose between a righteous God and a sinful soul. I saw at last a peradventure of hope, but on every other side I was surrounded with black, unfathomable despair.

"We found that all the casks of provision had been beaten to pieces by the violent motion of the ship. The sails, too, were mostly blown away. Thus we proceeded with an alternate prevalence of hopes and fears. My leisure time was chiefly employed in reading and meditating on the Scripture and praying to the Lord for mercy and instruction.

"Our stations was such as deprived us of any hope of being relieved by other vessels. The half of a salted cod was day's subsistence for twelve people. We had no bread, hardly any clothes, and very cold weather. We had incessant labor with the pumps to keep the ship above water. Much labor and little food wasted us fast, and one man died under the hardship. We had a terrible prospect of being either starved to death or reduced to feed upon one another. The captain, quite soured by distress, was hourly reproaching me as the sole cause of the calamity, and was confident that if I was thrown overboard, and not otherwise, they should be preserved from death (cp. Jonah). The continual repetition of this in my ears gave me much uneasiness, especially as my conscience seconded his words; I thought I was found out by the powerful hand of God, and condemned in my own breast.

"Thus it continued till we were called up to see land, and the next day anchored in Ireland. About this time I began to know there is a God that hears and answers prayer. The straits of hunger, cold, weariness, and the fears of sinking and starving, I shared in common with others; but besides these I felt a heart-bitterness which was properly my own. I always, till this time, hardened my neck still more and more after every reproof.

"As to books, I had a New Testament. In perusing it I was struck with several passages, particularly the prodigal, Luke 15, a case I thought had never been so nearly exemplified as by myself; this intended only to illustrate the Lord's goodness to returning sinners. I continued much in prayer; I saw that the Lord had interposed so far to save me.

"Before we arrived in Ireland I had satisfactory evidence in my own mind of the truth of the Gospel. I saw that by the way there pointed out, God might declare, not His mercy only, but His justice also, in the pardon of sin on account of the obedience and suffering of Jesus Christ. I stood in need of an almighty Savior, and such a One I found described in the New Testament. Thus far the Lord had wrought a marvelous thing: I was sincerely touched with a sense of the undeserved mercy I had received. Thus to all appearance, I was a new man."

We may fittingly close this account by quoting the oft-cited epitaph which John Newton wrote for himself and which was duly inscribed on his tomb: "*John Newton,* Clerk, once an infidel and libertine, a servant of slaves in Africa, was, by the rich mercy of our Lord and Savior, *Jesus Christ,* preserved, restored, pardoned, and appointed to preach the faith he had long labored to destroy."

25

MARTHA SNELL NICHOLSON:
God's Poet

On a bright Sunday in August, 1956, I was asked to preach in a little church close to Lomita, California. With no plans for the afternoon, we were asked if we would be interested in driving over to Wilmington where Martha Snell Nicholson was spending her declining days. We wondered if this would not be an unwarranted intrusion, but we were assured that, although Mrs. Nicholson could not enter into any protracted conversation, she would be happy for a quiet visit. Her housekeeper at the time assured us of the same thing, Mrs. Nicholson now being utterly helpless, and it proved to be but ten months before her release from a life of long and increasingly severe bodily pain.

Afflicted with such intense suffering year after year, those who knew her marveled at her unfailing cheerfulness, but most outstanding was her confidence in and love for the Lord. As her physical condition worsened, she still just rested in Him. When we saw her, her emaciated frame was grotesquely contorted by arthritis from which she suffered for years, in addition to tuberculosis, ankylosed spine, angina, Parkinson's disease, and finally cancer! Her calmness and undimmed love for the Lord put us to shame.

Martha Snell Nicholson possessed a gift from the Lord to write poems which were an encouragement and comfort to thousands. In spite of painful illness which kept her bedridden for the most part of twenty-nine years, she carried on her writing and composed over nine hundred poems, numbers of which have appeared in leading Christian magazines across the land. With the help of her husband, seven volumes were put out from their California home, and Mr. Nicholson, who died some nine years before her ministry was ended (another severe blow to her), reported, "We have distributed over a million of the leaflets carrying her poems." (I have many of them, plus two hardback volumes of selected poems put out by Moody Press after her Homegoing.)

Not everyone has a sudden conversion; some very devout Christians are unable to pinpoint the time and place when they stepped over the invisible line that separates between being lost and saved. Influences here and there doubtless have helped along the way, and some may be able to look back at elements later recognized as used by Holy Spirit in effecting their conversion. It may be encouraging to read of one not suddenly converted, but one about whose fullness in the Christian life there cannot be the slightest doubt.

Mrs. Nicholson wrote a deeply moving autobiography, *His Banner Over Me* (Moody Press, Chicago), which alludes to her coming to know Christ as a young person. These are the highlights of that wonderful knowledge:

"My mother always sang about the house as she worked. God pity children who do not have singing parents. I memorized dozens of the old hymns from hearing my parents sing them. I have no voice, but the words were stored in my heart years ago and have enriched me beyond measure . . .

"What is life without God? Pointless, fruitless, unfinished, actually not yet begun. I do not know the day nor the way God in His great graciousness and tenderness made Himself known to me. I wish that I could remember. I must have been six or seven when the tremendous event transpired and I became—as well the daughter of Mr. and Mrs. Snell—a child of the living God.

"Not only a child of God, but a joint-heir with Christ! All His riches became my riches. My sins were washed away in the precious blood of Christ. I had a great High Priest who would pray for me and present me faultless before the throne of God. I had the promise that nothing could ever touch me without His permission, the absolute certainty of a heavenly Home lovely beyond all my dreams of beauty, where I would dwell forever through eternity.

"I only knew that my passionate little heart was flooded with love for God and especially for the Lord Jesus. I loved Him so, that I thought of Him by day and dreamed of Him by night. The Bible tells us that when a sinner repents there is joy in Heaven. But when a small child puts her hand in His before too many mistakes have been made, before too many pages of life's book have been spoiled, then the angels must throng the very parapets of Heaven to look over and rejoice.

"A small, lonely soul venturing for the first time into the vast realms of the infinite cannot be satisfied with something dim and distant. The heart's deep cry is for someone near and dear with whom to tread these paths. And so, my Lord and I began to walk together, my hand resting trustingly in His."

———————————

Taken from the book, *His Banner Over Me* by Martha Snell Nicholson. Copyright © 1953 Moody Press. Used by permission of Moody Press.

26

PANDITA RAMABAI:
A High Caste Brahmin Finds Christ

In a Bible college with a strong missionary emphasis, we became acquainted with what were regarded as worthy missionary enterprises. Among those so recognized was one known as the Ramabai Mukti Mission of India, founded by Pandita Ramabai.

In a family conversation years ago, I let slip the name of this noted lady who established a truly remarkable work. My mother, who graduated from the University of California in 1899, remarked with enthusiasm that she had heard Pandita Ramabai speak in those early years at the University. This increased my interest in that lady's life—wondering how she happened to be given the opportunity to address a university in the United States, and even more, how she happened to become a Christian.

With many we have known, the usual pattern seems to be to become a Christian in some far off land and then to come to Western countries promoting interest in the needs of the homeland represented. In the case of Pandita Ramabai, however, the pattern evidently was the reverse. The Pandita appears to have been endowed by nature with a strong and brilliant character—an outstanding personality which made her acceptable wherever her early wide-ranging interests led her. Before long those interests directed her to the Western world and to a well-grounded knowledge of Christ. Here the intriguing story can only be told most briefly.

Dr. Robert Hall Glover, in *The Progress of World-Wide Missions,* declares, "The best known and most worthy of all is Pandita Ramabai, universally acknowledged to be the most distinguished woman in India, native or foreign. Her education was so thorough and her intellectual ability so great that the highest title possible for a native woman was conferred upon her. Forsaking idolatry, she turned to Christ and then consecrated herself with a love and devotion truly wonderful to the emancipation of child-wives and child-widows from their bondage. In later years her ministry expanded far beyond her original design, as she threw herself into the desperate situation and rescued thousands of girls and women from death, destitution and the base designs of wicked men . . .

"Her schools, orphanage and rescue home have witnessed some wonderful outpourings of the Holy Spirit and the conversion of great numbers of souls. After more than thirty years of prodigious labor, this great 'scholar, saint and servant,' as one of her biographers designates her, fell asleep in Jesus on April 5, 1922. Her death was noted in both the secular and the religious press the world around, and a host of her friends of every race deeply mourned her loss . . . Thousands of lives (were) touched and changed by her direct ministry, and other thousands inspired by her noble example."

John C. Thiessen's *A Survey of World Missions* gives a few more facts of her background. "This gifted woman of the Brahman caste had a father who—contrary to all Indian custom—taught his wife and daughters to read. Both parents died of starvation in the famine of 1876-77. Left to herself, Ramabai was married to a Bengali lawyer when she was twenty-two. After nineteen months he died of cholera, leaving her with a young daughter. In the desire to find peace for her soul, Ramabai undertook long and arduous pilgrimages."

Going on toward the matter of her conversion, J. Herbert Kane, in *Faith Mighty Faith,* relates, "From the time she was a young child, Ramabai and her brother accompanied their father— a Brahman priest—on long and arduous pilgrimages to the famous Hindu shrines of India. Year in and year out, they traveled the length and breadth of India, visiting sacred places, climbing sacred mountains, bathing in sacred rivers—all in search of peace. After the father died, Ramabai and her brother continued the search, walking four thousand miles on foot and eating only what the people were pleased to give them. Sometimes they went for days without food. During the cold Himalayan nights, Ramabai used to dig a shallow pit and blanket her brother with sand. Then she would dig a second pit for herself and crawl into it as best she could and cover herself with sand to keep from freezing. As she approached each new shrine she thought to herself, 'Maybe I will find peace here.' But peace did not come.

"One day, in the providence of God, she was led to Calcutta, and there she met some reformed Indians who took her to a meeting. It was all very strange to Ramabai, and she could not quite make it out. After reading from a book, the people knelt down in front of their chairs and began to mumble to the chairs. She thought they must be praying but she could see no images or idols, and wondered what it was all about. She was, however, struck by the apparent peace these people seemed to have and the joy with which they worshipped their gods. This was Ramabai's first contact with Christianity.

"It was not long before Ramabai learned that the Book was the Bible, and that the two venerable men who presided at the meeting had translated it into her native tongue. Being an educated woman, Ramabai was intensely interested in the Book whose words had already gripped her heart. She requested, and was given, a copy of the Bible which she cherished as long as she lived."

We continue the story from a biography, *Pandita Ramabai,* by Helen S. Dyer. "Ever since the death of her brother, and more particularly again after her husband died, Ramabai had felt in an undefined manner that God was guiding her. Disillusioned by painful experiences during her girlhood from the superstitions of Hinduism, she was still working from the Hindu standpoint. She knew but little of Christianity, and had no thought of becoming a Christian. Her mind became possessed of a divine unrest; and given the opportunity, she one day found herself bound for England— going forth, as she says, like Abraham, not knowing whither she went.

"Arriving in England with her baby daughter, Ramabai was kind-

ly received by a Church of England Sisterhood at Wantage . . . At
Wantage, time and opportunity to study the subject were afforded,
and here Ramabai confessed herself a Christian and was baptized
with her little daughter . . .

"The difference that Ramabai at the time discerned between the
good precepts of the Hindu scriptures and the gospel of Jesus Christ
she thus expressed: 'While the old Hindu scriptures have given us
some beautiful precepts of loving, the New Dispensation of Christ
has given us the grace to carry these principles into practice, and that
makes all the difference in the world. The precepts are like a steam
engine on the track, beautiful and with great possibilities; Christ and
His gospel are the steam, the motive power that can make the engine
move.'"

27

IRA SANKEY:
D. L. Moody's Talented Teammate

The well-known names, Moody and Sankey, have long been associated with notable evangelistic efforts in America and the British Isles. The first named, Moody, did the preaching, and much has been written about him. About the second, Sankey, not so much has been known among us, and this causes us to consider whether he is not worthy of more attention.

Who of us has not thrilled to the tune of *Faith Is The Victory,* or *The Ninety And Nine,* or *Under His Wings,* or *When The Mists Have Rolled Away*—all tunes written by Ira D. Sankey? And not only the music, but both words and music of *A Shelter In The Time Of Storm* were by him. A talented man was this, but more—a natural talent wholly consecrated to God for His use.

Mr. Sankey was, indeed, a vital part of the famous team, contributing not only in music, but by an attractive, winsome personality, and more, by the deep spirituality he imparted on the meetings. And he showed his modesty by willingly staying in the shadows.

Upon their arrival in England, some laughed at Sankey and his portable "suit-case" organ. By ultra-conservative and tradition-bound worshipers it was even called "the devil's box of whistles." But when crowds of ordinary people flocked to hear their presentations, and hearts were moved, no further justification was necessary.

A remarkable example of how Mr. Sankey was sometimes led is found in the composing of the tune of what is perhaps his best remembered and still much loved hymn, *The Ninety And Nine.* The story of how it came about has frequently been related, and accounts with minor variations may be found in a number of hymn-story books. It seems that Mr. Moody and Sankey were traveling by train to special meetings in Scotland. On the way, Sankey bought a newspaper, hoping for some news about America. He did not find much of what he sought, but by chance his eyes fell upon a poem in a corner of the paper, *The Ninety And Nine.* He himself said, "I at once made up my mind that this would make a great hymn for evangelistic work—if it had a tune." He casually clipped it and put it in his pocket.

About two days later Moody preached a gripping sermon on "The Good Shepherd." At its conclusion he turned to Sankey and asked, "Have you a solo appropriate for this subject, with which to close the service?" Sankey relates, "I had nothing suitable in mind and was greatly troubled to know what to do." But he seemed to hear an inner voice saying, "Sing the piece you found on the train." He drew it from his pocket and laid it on the organ. "I lifted my heart in prayer, asking God to help me . . . Laying my hands upon the organ I struck the key of A flat, and began to sing. Note by note the tune was given," which has not changed from that day to this.

As to Mr. Sankey's conversion, after searching through a number of volumes, it seemed no full account was available. Then I stumbled upon a rather large, musty volume, dated 1878, consisting mostly of D. L. Moody's early sermons, but in which also was found sketches of the lives of both Moody and Sankey. It reads in part:

"In the good providence of God, the gospel preacher [Moody] was given the gospel singer, that they might go forth together, like the first disciples sent out by the Lord—double in fellowship, single in heart—to labor as yoke-fellows in the harvest-field of the world. The first had been trained in the rugged school of adversity and self-denial. His companion, on the contrary, was reared under the hallowing influences of a happy Christian homestead, so that his whole character was mellowed by sweetening experiences of a childhood and manhood developed harmoniously and joyously. So strangely diverse was their training as individuals, yet so wisely ordered by the Master's hand.

"Ira D. Sankey's birthplace (1840) was in western Pennsylvania. His parents were members of the Methodist church. The father was well off in worldly circumstances, and in such good repute that they repeatedly elected him a member of the state legislature. He was also a licensed exhorter in his own church. Thus the means and the character of this household were such as to inspire ample advantages for culture in general knowledge and spiritual truth.

"Ira from his childhood was noted for his joyous spirit and trustful disposition. The sunshiny face that is so attractive in his public ministry has been a distinguishing feature from early boyhood . . . His father states, 'The gift of singing developed in him at a very early age. I say gift, because it was God-given. He never took lessons from anyone, but his taste for music was such that when a small boy he could make passable music on almost any kind of instrument.'

"An old Scotch farmer named Frazer early interested himself in the little lad; and of his good influence Mr. Sankey thus spoke at a children's meeting in Scotland: 'The very first recollection I have of anything pertaining to religious life was in connection with him. I remember he took me by the hand, along with his own boys, to the Sunday School—that old place which I shall remember to my dying day. He was a plain man, and I can see him standing up and praying for the children. He had a great, warm heart, and the children all loved him. It was years after that I was converted, but my impressions were received when I was very young, from that man.'

"Thus reared in a genial, religious atmosphere, liked and respected by all who knew him and accepted as a leader by his boyish companions, Ira lived on till past his fifteenth year before his soul was converted to Christ. His conviction as a sinner occurred while he attended a series of special services held in a little church three miles from his home. At first he was as carefree as his curious companions. But an earnest Christian met him each evening with a few soul-searching words; and after a week's hard struggle, he came as a sinner to the Savior and found peace in acceptance. Soon after, when his father removed to Newcastle to assume the presidency of the bank, Ira became a member of the Methodist Church.

"The young Christian was richly endowed with a talent for

singing spiritual songs. His pure, beautiful voice gave clear utterance to the emotions of his sympathetic, joyous nature, and was potent in carrying messages from his heart to the hearts of his hearers. It now became his delight to devote this precious gift to the service of his Lord, and it was his continual prayer that the Holy Spirit would bless the words he sang to the conversion of those who flocked to the services to hear him . . . His singing of the gospel invitations in solos dates from this time. The sweet hymns were sung in the very spirit of prayer, and the faith of the singer was rewarded with repeated blessings . . . The choir of the congregation also came under his leadership. He insisted on conduct befitting praise-singers in the house of God, and on a clear enunciation of each word sung."

As to Sankey's own singing, in *Eerdman's Handbook To The History Of Christianity,* we find the amazing statement, "It is said that fewer people listened to the works of Bach during the entire nineteenth century than heard Sankey sing in 1875."

On top of all else, Sankey was also noted for the repeated publication of songbooks. The authority just quoted says his *Sacred Songs and Solos* "grew from a sixpenny pamphlet (1873) to a book of 1200 pieces (1903)." And the *Wycliffe Biographical Dictionary of the Church* reports of this publication that "over fifty million copies were sold(!) The royalties were used for the support of the Christian institutions Moody established."

May God continue to give us gospel preaching and singing which is down-to-earth, but equally sound and soul-searching.

28

C. I. SCOFIELD:
Lawyer and Reference Bible Editor

C. I. Scofield is best remembered, over almost the whole world even of this day, for the reference Bible which he edited and which became to multitudes an inestimable help in understanding difficult and overlooked truths in the Word of God.

The story of Scofield's conversion has often been told, but perhaps the most authentic account is that found in *The Life Story of C. I. Scofield* by C. G. Trumbull (New York, Oxford University Press, 1920; Loizeaux Brothers, Inc., Neptune, NJ, current copyright holder), on which the following is based.

The family in which C. I. Scofield grew up was Episcopalian. The boy's father and mother were true Christians, old-fashioned believers. His father read the Bible to him and encouraged him to read it for himself.

The mother died soon after his birth. As she lay dying, the newborn baby boy by her side, she prayed for him and asked God that he might be a minister of the gospel. As the boy grew up, he was not told this; the father, with a strict sense of honor, told the sisters that young Cyrus must not be told of his mother's prayer lest he be unduly influenced by it and enter upon a life calling simply because of sentiment and from a sense of obligation to a dying mother's wish. Only after that boy had accepted the call to the ministry was he told of his mother's prayer.

The Scofields were living in Tennessee when the Civil War came on. Enlisting, though only seventeen at the time, he saw several years' service. Under fire in eighteen battles and minor engagements, he was awarded the Cross of Honor.

Scofield studied law as opportunity afforded, finally was admitted to the bar, and then the people of Atchison, Kansas elected him to the state legislature. Later, General Grant, then President of the United States for his second term, appointed C. I. Scofield United States Attorney for the District of Kansas, which at that time included much outlying Indian territory. The young legislator was the youngest United States attorney in the country at that time.

Still later he settled into a law practice at St. Louis. He had been living not at all as a Puritan. The moderate use of liquor was commonplace in the life in which he moved. He drank as he pleased, and, like most men who drink "in moderation," he soon drank too much.

In his law practice, a young man of about his own age, Tom McPheeters, became one of his intimate friends. McPheeters was the son of a godly man of great influence.

Scofield's father and mother had been true believers. He was not. He had gone to Sunday school as a boy because he was made to go. He hated to go; it made little impression upon him; and he learned little there. He heard many a sermon but none that affected him in any way.

In his St. Louis law office one day, McPheeters came to see him. After talking awhile, McPheeters got up to go. With his hand upon the doorknob, he turned and faced Scofield, saying: "For a long time I have been wanting to ask you a question that I have been afraid to ask but that I am going to ask you now."

"I never thought of you as 'afraid,'" said Scofield in hearty friendship. "What is your question?"

"I want to ask you why you are not a Christian?" came the unexpected reply.

Now Tom McPheeters was an outspoken Christian himself, utterly devoted to his Lord. He and Scofield had much in common—except Christ.

The lawyer replied thoughtfully: "Does not the Bible say

something about drunkards having no place in Heaven? I am a hard drinker, McPheeters."

"You haven't answered my question, Scofield," the other man came back. "Why are you not a Christian?"

"I have always been an nominal Episcopalian, you know," said Scofield, "but I do not recall ever having been shown just how to be a Christian."

Now McPheeters had his answer. He drew up a chair, took a Testament out of his pocket and read passage after passage from the precious Good News, plainly telling his friend how to be saved. "Will you accept the Lord Jesus Christ as your Savior?" he asked.

"I'm going to think about it," said Scofield.

"No, you're not," answered McPheeters. "You've been thinking about it all your life. Will you settle it now? Will you believe on Christ now and be saved?"

The logical-minded, clear-thinking lawyer liked clean-cut statements and unequivocal questions and answers. After a moment's thought he looked his friend full in the face and said quietly, "I will." The two men dropped down on their knees together. Scofield told the Lord Jesus Christ that he believed on Him as his personal Savior, and before he arose from his knees he had been born again; there was a new creation, old things had passed away, behold all things had become new. Tom McPheeters had been used of God to lead C. I. Scofield to Christ.

Lawyer Scofield was saved, and he knew it for Thomas McPheeters knew the gospel and had made it perfectly plain to his friend. There was no vagueness or uncertainty in McPheeter's appeal nor in Scofield's acceptance. From that day he never had any doubt that he was at that time, in the city of St. Louis, born again through faith in the Son of God.

Years later, Dr. Scofield wanted to make it very emphatic, so in a letter he wrote: " . . . slowly, insidiously, the all but universal habit of drink in the society and among the men of my time over-mastered me. I was a ruined and hopeless man who, despite all his struggles, was fast bound in chains of his own forging . . . From a worn pocket Testament McPheeters read to me the great gospel passages. We knelt, and I received Jesus Christ as my Savior. Instantly the chains were broken, never to be forged again—the passion for drink was taken away. Divine power did it, wholly of grace. To Christ be all the glory."

29

A. B. SIMPSON:
Founder of The Christian & Missionary Alliance

Albert B. Simpson (1843-1919) will long be recognized for having brought together what came to be known as the Christian and Missionary Alliance. Not started as a new denomination, yet its local churches have sprung up far and wide across the globe. Especially it is recognized for its extensive worldwide missionary endeavors.

Ruth Tucker, in *From Jerusalem to Irian Jaya,* says of Simpson, "His influence for missions was enormous . . . Largely through his influence, foreign missions in the twentieth century became the most vital outreach of the North American evangelical churches." Then she speaks of him as "becoming America's foremost missionary statesman . . . His missionary training school concept launched the Bible Institute movement that spread out across North America and became the major recruiting source for independent faith mission societies in the decades that followed."

J. Gilchrist Lawson, in *Famous Missionaries,* adds this interesting sidelight: "It is estimated that Dr. Simpson administered over six million dollars and opened over four hundred stations in sixteen different mission fields . . . He wrote many books and over three hundred hymns."

Simpson also displayed "exceptional preaching ability" (Tucker). It is reported that D. L. Moody "said to his friend, A. T. Pierson, 'I have just been down to hear A. B. Simpson preach. No one gets at my heart like that man.'" (*A. B. Simpson,* by A.E. Thompson). And C. I. Scofield is reported to have said, "Among the greater preachers and men of God of the present time . . . I count Dr. A. B. Simpson the foremost in power to reach the depths of the human soul . . . With this seasoned and mature gift was united a power of detail and of organization that made him unique among the great Christian leaders of the day" (Thompson).

In the index volume of Dr. W. B. Riley's 40-volume set, *The Bible of the Expositor and Evangelist,* we find ten different citations from A. B. Simpson. To give just one example, Riley introduces a long excerpt from Simpson, saying, "Dr. A. B. Simpson has a little tract on 'Himself' that I wish every Christian might read." No wonder much is found in his writings, for it is said Simpson "wrote more than seventy books" (Thompson).

Showing what a well rounded-out man Simpson was, we read, "It is needless to recount the many activities—his pulpit and platform work, his pastoral duties, his ministry for the sick, his lectures in the Institute, his convention tours, his correspondence, his editorial labors, his preparation of books, his production of hymns, and his executive responsibilities" (Thompson). He edited the first illustrated missionary magazine on the American continent.

Even more remarkable, to us at least, is the place Dr. Wilbur M. Smith affords Simpson's writing. In *Profitable Bible Study,* Dr. Smith presents his carefully selected and widely acclaimed list of "The First One Hundred Books for the Bible Student's Library" (1939, revised edition, 1953). In that rigidly limited list of top recommendations is a work by A. B. Simpson: *The Holy Spirit, or Power from on High.* On this Dr. Smith says in part, "We believe that of all the works on the Holy Spirit . . . this will be found by Bible teachers and ministers the most satisfactory. Dr. Simpson had a profound knowledge of the Word of God, and was a truly great preacher, and lived a godly life." Finally, Dr. Smith says, "Personally, I do not believe that Dr. Simpson can be followed in some of his interpretations; still I recommend this work heartily."

Perhaps contributing to his greatness was the fact that things did not always come easily or go smoothly for A. B. Simpson. Many a time he was distraught and anguished over the struggle in which he found himself. Even his assurance of salvation did not come easily. We tell it in his own words, taken from Thompson's biography.

"My father was a good Presbyterian elder of the old school, and believed in the Shorter Catechism, the doctrine of foreordination, and all the conventional principles of a well ordered Puritan household . . . I had no personal hope in Christ. My whole religious training had left me without any conception of the sweet and simple gospel of Jesus Christ . . . There was no voice to tell me the simple way of believing in the promise and accepting the salvation fully provided and freely offered. How often since then it has been my delight to tell poor sinners that 'We do not need at mercy's gate to knock and weep and watch and wait, for mercy's free gifts are offered free, and she has waited long for thee.'

"My life seemed to hang upon a thread, for I had the hope that God would spare me long enough to find salvation. One day in the library of my old minister and teacher, I stumbled upon an old musty volume. As I turned the leaves, my eyes fell upon a sentence which opened for me the gates of life eternal. It is this in substance: 'The first good work you will ever perform is to believe on the Lord Jesus Christ. Until you do this, all your works, prayers, tears, and good resolutions are vain. To believe on the Lord Jesus is just to believe that He saves you according to His Word, that He receives and saves you here and now, for He has said—"Him that cometh to me I will in no wise cast out." The moment you do this you will pass into eternal life, you will be justified from all your sins, and receive a new heart.' . . .

"To my poor bewildered soul this was like the light from heaven that fell upon Saul of Tarsus on his way to Damascus. I immediately fell upon my knees, and looking up to the Lord, I said, 'Lord Jesus, Thou hast said, "Him that cometh to me I will in no wise cast out." Thou knowest how long and earnestly I have tried to come, but I did not know how. Now I come the best I can, and I dare to believe that Thou dost receive me and save me, and that I am now Thy child, forgiven and saved simply because I have taken Thee at Thy word.'

"I had a fight of faith with the great Adversary before I was able to get out all these words and dared to make this confession of my faith; but I had no sooner made it and set my seal to it than there came to my heart that divine assurance that always comes to the believing soul . . .

"The months that followed my conversion were full of spiritual blessing. The promises of God burst upon my soul with a new and marvelous light, and words that had been empty before became divine revelations and seemed especially meant for me."

Thus Albert B. Simpson began where any sincere soul may begin; that is, at the starting line of simple faith. May many more begin at the same point.

30

RODNEY "GIPSY" SMITH:
God's Evangelist

Gipsy Smith was a very commonplace, homespun individual coming from a humble and unlettered background, but it was my privilege to hear him in one of the most ornate and pretentious churches in southern California many years ago. He rose to a level of culture and learning recognized by all. He commanded the respect of very class, always the perfect gentleman despite lowly origins. A sense of warmth, pleasant humor, and earnestness marked his preaching. He blessed multitudes in repeated trips from his native England to America—as well as to South Africa, Australia, and other lands.

The following account of his conversion is taken from *Gipsy Smith's Best Sermons* (The Brooklyn Eagle, 1907), and from his *Autobiography* (Revell, 1902).

"My father had become a Christian. The light came to him at my mother's death. He was left alone with five small children, and the parting words of my mother were: 'Take care of the little ones. Beloved, take care of our children.' And there was my father—a big, strong man—who, without a Bible, without a teacher, without a guiding hand, without knowing how to read or write, came to God. . . .

"We were traveling in our wagon through Hertfordshire,

England, when my sister—the eldest of the children—was taken ill. We drove up to the doctor's house. He said, 'It is smallpox; you must go away from here.' We went to a by-place called Norton Lane. There my father pitched our tent, where he left my mother and the four other children. The wagon he placed two hundred yards or more away, and there he went with the sick child, whom he nursed and cared for. In a few days my brother, Ezekiel, was taken down with the smallpox and he, too, was sent to the wagon. My mother carried the food she prepared for the invalids half way between the wagon and the tent, when she would call for my father. Sometimes he was busily engaged with his little charges and the snow would get on the food, and my mother, in her anxiety for her children, would get nearer and nearer to the wagon, and one day she, too, had smallpox.

"There in the forest was Gipsy Smith's father with his dying wife and little children. With no knowledge of the Bible, with little knowledge of God, he reached out to the dying woman.

"'Do you believe in God?' he asked.

"'Yes,' answered the woman.

"'Do you try to pray, beloved?' he asked.

"'I try to,' answered the woman . . .

"The woman put her arms around his neck and kissed him. He went outside and wept, and he heard her singing:

'I have a father in the promised land;

My God calls me, I must go to meet him . . .'

"It was a song she had heard twenty years before, sung by school children. It came to her as her life ebbed out.

"I shall never forget that day my father came to me and said, 'Rodney, you have no mother' . . .

"Although I was a mischievous boy, I knew in my heart what religion meant. I had seen it in the new lives of my father, sisters, and brother. I had seen the transformation-scene if I had not felt it, and in my heart there was a deep longing for the strange experiences which I knew to be my father's.

"I remember well a visit that my father paid to Bedford about that time. I shall never forget my thoughts and feelings while I listened to the people as they spoke of John Bunyan. They took us to see the church where he used to preach and showed us his monument. During our stay in the town, I spent some portion of every day near the monument. I had heard the people say he had been a tinker [*as Smith's father was*] and a great sinner, but had been converted, and that through his goodness he became great. And, oh! how I looked up as he stood on that pedestal and longed to be good like him. And I wondered if I should always live in a 'wagon' and spend a life of uselessness. I walked to the village where John Bunyan was born and went into the house he had lived in. I stood and wept and longed to find the same Jesus Christ that had made Bunyan what he was. I never lost sight in my mind's eye of the bright visions that visited me while I was in Bedford.

"I remember one evening sitting on the trunk of an old tree not far from my father's tent and wagon. Around the fallen trunk grass had grown about as tall as myself. I had gone there to think and, because I was under the deepest conviction, had an earnest longing to love the Savior and to be a good lad. I thought of my mother in Heaven, and I thought of the beautiful life my father, brother, and sisters were living, and I said to myself, 'Rodney, are you going to wander about as a gipsy boy and a gipsy man without hope, or will you be a Christian and have some definite object to live for?' Everything was still, and I could almost hear the beating of my heart. For answer to my question, I found myself startling myself by my own voice: 'By the grace of God, I will be a Christian and I will meet my mother in Heaven!' My decision was made. I believe I was as much accepted by the Lord Jesus that day as I am now, for with all my heart I had decided to live for Him. My choice was made forever . . .

"A few days afterwards I wandered one evening into a little Primitive Methodist Chapel in Fitzroy Street, Cambridge, where I heard a sermon by the Rev. George Warner. Oddly enough, I cannot remember a word of what Mr. Warner said, but I made up my mind in that service that if there was a chance I would publicly give myself to Christ. After the sermon a prayer meeting was held, and Mr. Warner invited all those who desired to give themselves to the Lord to come forward and kneel at the communion rail. I was the first to go forward. I do not know whether anybody else was there or not. I think not. While I prayed the congregation sang. Soon there was a dear old man beside me, an old man with great flowing locks, who put his arm around me and began to pray with me and for me. I did not know his name. I do not know it even now. I told him that

I had given myself to Jesus for time and eternity—to be his boy forever. He said:

"'You must believe that He has saved you. "To as many as received Him, to them gave He power to be the sons of God; even to them that believed on His name."'

"'Well,' I said to my dear old friend, 'I cannot trust myself, for I am nothing, and I cannot trust in what I have, for I have nothing; and I cannot trust in what I know, for I know nothing; and so far as I can see, my friends are as badly off as I am.'

"So there and then I placed myself by simple trust and committal to Jesus Christ. I knew He died for me, I knew He was able to save me, and I just believed Him to be as good as His word. And thus the light broke and assurance came. I went home and told my father that his prayers were answered, and he wept with tears of joy with me . . .

"Next morning I had, of course, as usual to go out and sell my goods. My first desire was to see again the little place where I had kneeled the night before ere I commenced my work for the day. There I stood for some minutes gazing at the little chapel, almost worshiping the place. As I stood, I heard a shuffling of feet, and turning round I saw the dear old man who had knelt by my side. I said to myself, 'Now that I have my goods—clothes-pegs and tinware—with me, he will see that I am a gipsy, and will not take any notice of me. He will not speak to a gipsy boy. Nobody cares for me but my father.' But I was quite wrong. Seeing me, he remembered me at once, and came over to speak to me, though he walked with great difficulty. Taking my hands in his, he seemed to look right down into my innermost soul. Then he said to me, 'The Lord bless you, my boy. The Lord keep you, my boy.' I wanted to thank him, but the words would not come. There was a lump in my throat. The dear old man passed on, and I watched him turning the corner out of my sight forever. I never saw him again. But when I reach the glory-land, I will find out that dear old man, and I will thank that grand old saint for his shake of the hand and for his 'God bless you!' For he made me feel that somebody outside the tent really cared for a gipsy boy's soul."

31

CHARLES HADDON SPURGEON:
Prince of Preachers

The name of Charles Haddon Spurgeon is so well-known that little need be said to remind us of the great London preacher. While his Metropolitan Tabernacle (seating six thousand) was being built, his congregation moved to "Surrey Music Hall where he preached to audiences numbering ten thousand people. At twenty-two the most popular preacher of his day" (*Wycliffe Biographical Dictionary of the Church*). Though he died in 1892, "His sermons were published weekly until 1917. He was the most popular and the greatest preacher of his age" (*Eerdman's Handbook to the History of Christianity*). His influence not being confined to the pulpit, his "writing reached an enormous circulation . . . Published more than two thousand sermons. Forty-nine-volume set of the *Metropolitan Pulpit* was a mammoth work" (*Wycliffe*, op. cit.). He published other volumes, founded orphanages, a Bible society, a pastors' college, branch churches, etc. He was a friend and backer of D. L. Moody. Although a leader among the Baptists, he was respected by all; as a Church of England clergyman put it:

"There was an old preacher named Spurgey,
He had no use for liturgy,

But his sermons were fine, I take them for mine,
And so does the rest of the clergy."

Although titular head of the Church of England, rumor had it that Queen Victoria, in disguise, went to hear him once.

The story of Spurgeon's conversion is taken as related, first, in his life, *"From The Usher's Desk To The Tabernacle Pulpit,"* and from a leaflet, *"How Spurgeon Found Christ,"* by himself, which has gone through many editions. In his own words:

"I will tell you how I myself was brought to the knowledge of the truth. It may happen that the telling of it will bring someone else to Christ. It pleased God in my childhood to convince me of sin. I lived a miserable creature, finding no hope, no comfort, thinking that surely God would never save me. At last the worst came to the worst—I was miserable.

"I resolved that, in the town where I lived, I would visit every place of worship in order to find out the way of salvation. I felt I was willing to do anything and be anything if God would only forgive me. I set off, determined to go round to all the chapels, and I went to all the places of worship; and though I dearly venerate the men, I am bound to say that I never heard them once fully preach the gospel. I mean by that, they preached truth, great truths, many good truths that were fitting to many of their congregations, but what I wanted to know was, how can I get my sins forgiven? And they never told me that. I wanted to hear how a poor sinner, under a sense of sin, might find peace with God. I went time after time, and I am sure there was not a more attentive hearer in all the place than myself, for I panted and longed to understand how I might be saved.

"The secret of my distress was this: I did not know the gospel. I was in a Christian land, I had Christian parents, but I did not fully understand the freeness and simplicity of the gospel. I attended all the places of worship in the town where I live, but I honestly believe that I did not hear the gospel fully preached. One man preached the divine sovereignty. But what was that to a poor sinner who wished to know what he should do to be saved? There was another admirable man who always preached about the law. Another was a great practical preacher. I heard him, but it was very much like a commanding officer teaching the maneuvers of war to a set of men without feet.

"I sometimes think I might have been in darkness and despair now had it not been for the goodness of God in sending a snowstorm one Sunday morning when I was going to a place of worship. When I could go no further, I turned down a court and came to a little Primitive Methodist chapel. In that chapel there might be a dozen or fifteen people. The minister did not come that morning—snowed up, I suppose. A poor man, a shoemaker, a tailor or something of that sort, went up into the pulpit to preach.

"Now it is well that ministers should be instructed, but this man was really stupid, as you would say. He was obliged to stick to his text for the simple reason that he had nothing else to say. The text was 'Look unto me, and be ye saved, all the ends of the earth' (Isa. 45:22). He did not even pronounce the words rightly, but that did not matter.

"There was, I thought, a gleam of hope for me in the text. He began thus: 'My dear friends, this is a very simple text indeed. It says, Look. Now that does not take a deal of effort. It ain't lifting your foot or your finger; it is just "look." Well, a man need not go to college to learn to look. A man need not be worth a thousand a year to look. Anyone can look; a child can look. But this is what the text says. Then it says, "Look unto me." Ay,' said he, 'many on ye are looking to yourselves. No use looking there. You'll never find comfort in yourselves. Jesus Christ says, "Look unto me." Some of you say, "I must wait the Spirit's working." You have no business with that just now. Look to *Christ*. It runs "Look unto Me."'

"When he had managed to spin out ten minutes or so, he was at the end of his tether. Then he looked at me under the gallery, and I dare say, with so few present, he knew me to be a stranger. He then said, 'Young man, you look very miserable.' Well I did, but I had not been accustomed to have remarks made on my personal appearance from the pulpit before. However, it was a good blow struck. He continued: 'And you will always be miserable—miserable in life and miserable in death—if you do not obey my text. But if you obey now, this moment you will be saved.'

"Then he shouted as only a Primitive Methodist can, 'Young man, look to Jesus Christ!' I did look. There and then the cloud was gone, the darkness had rolled away, and that moment I saw the sun; I could have risen that moment and sung with the most enthusiastic of them of the precious blood of Christ and the simple faith which looks alone to Him. Oh, that somebody had told me that before: *Trust Christ, and you shall be saved.*

"I now think I am bound never to preach a sermon without preaching to sinners. I do think that a minister who can preach a sermon without addressing sinners does not know how to preach."

32

C. T. STUDD:
God's Cricketeer

C. T. Studd, the "famous cricketer" and one of the "Cambridge Seven," came from an English family of wealth and prestige. After serving as a missionary for a time in China and then India, he plunged into Central Africa where he founded the Heart of Africa Mission (now the Worldwide Evangelization Crusade). He labored there long after the usual retirement age, away from family and loved ones, camping in most primitive conditions. His story is told in N. P. Grubb's *C. T. Studd, Cricketer and Pioneer,* from which the following is taken.

First in Studd's own words: "I used to think that religion was a Sunday thing, like one's Sunday clothes, to be put away on Monday morning. We boys were brought up to go to church regularly; but, although we had a kind of religion, it didn't amount to much. It was just like having a toothache. We were always sorry to have Sunday come and glad when it was Monday morning. The Sabbath was the dullest day of the whole week, and just because we had gotten hold of the wrong end of religion. Then all at once I had the good fortune to meet a real live play-the-game Christian. It was my own father [who owned a large country estate, whose life was wrapped up in horse racing, and who experienced a remarkable conversion a short time before under D. L. Moody's ministry]. But it did make one's hair stand on end. All members of the household had a dog's life of it until they were converted. After a time I used to sham sleep when I saw the door open, and in the day I crept round the other side of the house when I saw him coming."

Grubb continues the story: "The boys were home for the summer holidays at Tedworth, and a number of cricket matches had been arranged. As usual, their father had men staying in the house each weekend to speak at the meetings on Sunday. Two were down one weekend, and one of them was popular with the boys; and the other, Mr. W., was not, for they considered him a 'milk-sop.' On the Saturday morning they planned a trick on him. They asked him to go for a ride with them and their father; for they had discovered that, although he said he could ride, he was really no good at it. The three boys rode behind and suddenly passed the other two, cantering like the wind; and of course, nothing could hold the horses—to the great discomfort of Mr. W. He, however, had more mettle than he appeared to have and kept his seat. They repeated this several times, and their father could not rebuke them because he was bursting with laughter himself.

"But that afternoon Mr. W. had his revenge. He spoke to all three boys individually and got them to surrender to Christ, each without the other knowing."

Studd tells what happened in his own words: "As I was going out to play cricket, he caught me unawares and asked, 'Are you a Christian?' I said, 'I am not what you call a Christian. I have believed in Jesus Christ since I was knee high. Of course, I believe in the Church, too.' I thought by answering him pretty close, I would get rid of him; but he stuck as tight as wax and said, 'Look here, *God so loved the world, that he gave his only begotten Son, that whosoever believeth on him should not perish, but have everlasting life.* You believe that Christ died?' 'Yes.' 'You believe He died for you?' 'Yes.' 'Do you believe the other half of the verse—"shall have everlasting life"?' 'No,' I said, 'I don't believe that.' He said, 'Now, don't you see that your statement contradicts God? Either God or you is not speaking the truth, for you contradict one another. Which is it? Do you think that God is a liar?' 'No,' I said. 'Well, then, aren't you inconsistent, believing one-half of the verse and not the other half?' 'I suppose I am.' 'Well,' he said, 'are you always going to be inconsistent?' 'No,' I said, 'I suppose not always.' He said,

'Will you be consistent now?' I saw that I was cornered; and I began to think, If I go out of this room inconsistent, I won't carry much self-respect. So I said, 'Yes, I will be consistent.' 'Well, don't you see that eternal life is a gift? When someone gives you a present, what do you do?' 'I take it and say, "thank you."' He said, 'Will you say "thank you" to God for this gift?' Then I got down on my knees, and I did say 'thank you' to God. And right then and there joy and peace came into my soul. I knew then what it was to be 'born again,' and the Bible, which had been so dry to me before, became everything."

Grubb concludes the story: "C. T. said nothing to his brothers at the time, but on returning to Eaton he wrote and told his father. Then a few days later at breakfast in their room at Eaton, he and his brothers received a joint letter from their father saying how glad he was to hear the good news. They got a big surprise as they passed the letter from one to the other and found that the three brothers had each made his decision on the same day. So the 'milk-sop' who was no good in games was really an expert at the greatest game of all—catching men for Christ, and he had hooked three shy fish, all members of the Eaton Eleven, in one day."

Taken from the book, *C. T. Studd* by Norman Grubb. Copyright ©1982 Christian Literature Crusade. Used by permission of Christian Literature Crusade.

33

BILLY SUNDAY:
Striking-Out the Devil

Those of us who listened to Billy Sunday preach can never forget his dynamic, impassioned manner. Even in his more mature years he would dash across the platform, jumping here and there, all the while using these movements, not to show off or entertain, but to emphasize important points he was making. Having been a famous baseball player, great crowds thronged to hear him after his conversion. And his sermons were not without solid content. Having heard the preaching of R. A. Torrey, H. A. Ironside, G. Campbell Morgan and other greats, as well as a religious address by William Jennings Bryan, I can say that one of the greatest single sermons to which I have ever listened—homiletically, for style of delivery and for solid content—was by Billy Sunday.

About fifteen years after having heard him (he having passed away), I was on the program of Winona Lake's Fiftieth Anniversary Jubilee celebration where I was introduced in the Billy Sunday Tabernacle to "Ma" Sunday, the grand old lady of Winona Lake. It is no wonder, then, that I have been interested in Billy's conversion, as have countless others, from the baseball world to those in common walks to the more erudite classes.

Sunday used to recount the story of his conversion in nearly every campaign. I gleaned it from three biographies I have long had,

143

those by Elijah P. Brown, William T. Ellis, and T. T. Frankenberg.

Frankenberg points out, "At the time of his conversion, Mr. Sunday had been a baseball player of national reputation for four years; he was in receipt of a salary which at the time was considered very large. As life goes, for men of that class, success and whatever happiness that is supposed to bring with it was already his . . . It is not to be presumed, therefore, that the conversion of the baseball player was predicated upon his previous religious activities other than that of his very early home days . . . In his daily occupation as a ballplayer, Sunday's life had become what is probably described by the world as "wild"—not vicious or corrupt, but still a departure from the rigid training of his boyhood days."

E. P. Brown recounts, "One Sunday afternoon Billy was strolling about in the south end of the business district of Chicago with half a dozen baseball friends. The New York Giants were in the city at the time, and several of them were in the party. At the corner of State and Van Buren Streets was an empty lot. Here a company of men and women workers from the Pacific Garden Mission were holding an outdoor meeting. Sunday and his friends stopped to listen."

Then, as Billy Sunday himself tells it as recorded in several sources: "I walked down a street in Chicago in company with some ballplayers who were famous in this world. We sat down on a corner. I never go by that street without thanking God for saving me. It was a vacant lot at the time. We sat down on a curbing. Across the street a company of men and women were playing on instruments— horns, flutes and slide trombones—and the others were singing the gospel hymns that I used to hear my mother sing back in the log cabin in Iowa and back in the old church where I used to go to Sunday school.

"And God painted on the canvas of my recollection and memory a vivid picture of the scenes of other days and other faces. Many have long since turned to dust.

"I sobbed and sobbed, and a young man stepped out and said, 'We are going down to the Pacific Garden Mission. Won't you come down to the mission? I am sure you will enjoy it. You can hear drunkards tell how they have been saved.' The ballplayers had been drinking.

"I arose and said to the boys, 'I'm through. We've come to the parting of the ways,' and I turned my back on them. Some of them laughed, and some of them mocked me; one of them gave me encouragement; others never said a word.

"I turned and left that little group on the corner, walked to the little mission and fell on my knees and staggered out of sin and into the arms of the Savior.

"The next day I had to get out to the ballpark and practice. Every morning at ten o'clock we had to be out there. I never slept that night. I was afraid of the horselaughs that gang would give me because I had taken my stand for Jesus Christ.

"I walked down to the old ball grounds. I will never forget it. The first man to meet me after I got inside was Mike Kelly. Up came Mike and said, 'Bill, I'm proud of you. Religion is not my long suit, but I'll help you all I can.' Up came Anson, the best ballplayer that ever played the game. There wasn't a fellow in that gang who knocked; every fellow had a word of encouragement for me . . . .

"Frank Flint, our old catcher who caught for nineteen years, drew $3,200-a-year on an average. He caught before they had chest protectors, masks and gloves. He caught bare-handed. Every bone in the ball of his hand was broken. Every bone in his face was broken, and his nose and cheekbones, and the shoulder and ribs had all been broken. He got to drinking, his home was broken up, and he went to the dogs.

"I've seen old Frank Flint sleeping on a table in a stale beer joint. He drank on and on, and one day in winter he staggered out of a stale beer joint and was seized with a fit of coughing. The blood streamed out of his nose, mouth and eyes. Down the street came a woman. She took one look and said, 'My God, is it you, Frank?' and his wife came up and kissed him. She called two policemen and a cab and started with him to her boardinghouse. They broke all speed regulations. She called five of the best physicians, and they listened to the beating of his heart, and the doctors said, 'He will be dead in about four hours.' She said, 'Frank, the end is near.' And he said, 'Send for Bill.'

"They telephoned me, and I came. He said, 'There's nothing in the life of years ago I care for now. I can hear the grandstand cheer. But there is nothing that can help me out now. If the Umpire calls me out now, won't you say a few words over me, Bill?' He struggled as he had years ago on the diamond, when he tried to reach home—but the great Umpire of the universe yelled, 'You're out!' and the great gladiator of the diamond was no more.

"He sat on the street corner with me, drunk, years ago in Chicago, when I said 'Good-by, boys, I'm through.' Did they win the game of life, or did I?"

Just a final note. In his 1917 evangelistic campaign in New York City, the meetings ran for ten weeks—a phenomenal record for such a campaign—and the thank-offering came to $120,482. Sunday gave the entire amount to overseas work among American soldiers during World War I. What a testimony!

34

J. HUDSON TAYLOR:
Opening China for the Gospel

We might not expect a history of Christian work in the United States to make mention of an Englishman and his mission, but *Eerdmans' Handbook To Christianity in America* recognizes J. Hudson Taylor's influence even on our continent. In part, it reports, "An Englishman, J. Hudson Taylor, launched the China Inland Mission which became the pattern for interdenominational 'faith' missions."

Another similar work, *Eerdmans' Handbook To The History Of Christianity,* states of Taylor's mission: "This was the first truly interdenominational foreign mission, and the prototype of the 'faith' missions that were to play so prominent a part in world evangelization during the nineteenth century . . . By his writing and preaching [Taylor] made a great impact during his lifetime."

Further aspects of the impact of Hudson Taylor's life are brought out by other writers. In *Introduction To Christian Missions,* T. C. Johnson, declares, "The zeal for missions has been made more widespread by certain movements such as the China Inland Mission founded by that genius of deep consecration, Dr. J. Hudson Taylor. It made little of educational but much of spiritual preparation. It sought missionaries who would be content with whatever God should supply . . . It made the essence of mission work not Christianizing but *evangelizing.*"

Approaching the matter of Hudson Taylor's conversion, A. W. Halsey, speaking at a great missionary conference in New York (April 30, 1900), said, "Hudson Taylor is only a man like the rest of us; yet no one can read the story of this man, from the hour when a lad of fifteen he was brought to Christ, while his mother, far away, spent the afternoon in prayer for him, to the moment when under the direct guidance of God he began in prayer and faith the China Inland Mission, and not be convinced."

The interesting details of that conversion have often been retold. For our purpose we take it from *Hudson Taylor: The Man Who Believed God,* by Marshall Broomhall (virtually the same is found in the larger biography by Mrs. Howard Taylor, and others).

Broomhall begins with the striking words, "Some time after Hudson Taylor's death, a distinguished editor wrote, 'If Hudson Taylor had been a statesman, there is no doubt whatever that he would have been reckoned one of the few greatest British statesmen of our time . . . If he had gone out to China with money and enterprise . . . covering that vast land with British traders, as he did cover it with British evangelists, his name would have been as familiar to the man in the street as the name of Cecil Rhodes. And yet his influence in China, and through China on the world, will be greater, and an influence, moreover, that is altogether good.' . . .

"When fourteen years of age, Hudson Taylor made his first definite surrender of himself to God. This was brought about through the reading of a leaflet published by the Religious Tract Society, and concerning this experience he wrote some few years later: 'From my earliest childhood I have felt the strivings of the Holy Spirit, and when about fourteen years of age I gave my heart to God.'

"Worldly associates made him for a time set his heart on wealth and worldly pleasures, and predisposed him towards skeptical and infidel teaching. He wrote, 'These views I retained when the Lord was pleased to bring me to Himself.'" We continue the story in Taylor's own words:

"Let me tell you how God answered the prayers of my dear mother and of my beloved sister, for my conversion. On a day which I shall never forget, my dear mother being absent from home, I had a holiday, and in the afternoon looked through my father's library to find some book with which to while away the unoccupied hours. Nothing attracting me, I turned over a little basket of pamphlets, and selected from among them a gospel tract which looked interesting, saying to myself, 'There will be a story at the commencement, and a sermon or moral at the close; I will take the former and leave the latter for those who like it.'

"I sat down to read the little book in an utterly unconcerned state of mind, believing indeed at the time that if there were any salvation it was not for me, and with a distinct intention to put away the tract as soon as it should seem prosy. I may say that it was not uncommon in those days to call conversion 'becoming serious.' Would it not be well to call conversion 'becoming joyful' instead of 'becoming serious'?

"Little did I know at the time what was going on in the heart of my mother, seventy or eighty miles away. She rose from the dinner table that afternoon with an intense yearning for the conversion of her boy, and feeling that—absent from home, and having more leisure than she could otherwise secure—a special opportunity was afforded her of pleading with God on my behalf. She went to her room and turned the key in the door, resolved not to leave that spot until her prayers were answered. Hour after hour did that dear mother plead for me, until at length she could pray no longer, but was constrained to praise God for that which His Spirit taught her had already been accomplished—the conversion of her only son.

"In the meantime I had been led to take up this little tract, and while reading it was struck with the sentence, 'The finished work of Christ.' The thought passed through my mind, 'Why does the author use this expression? Why not say the atoning or propitiatory work of Christ?' Immediately the words. 'It is finished' suggested themselves to my mind. What was finished? And I at once replied, 'A full and perfect atonement and satisfaction for sin; the debt was paid by the Substitute; Christ died for our sins, and not for ours only, but for the sins of the whole world.' Then came the thought, 'If the whole work was finished and the whole debt paid, what is there left for me to do?' And with this dawned the joyful conviction, as light was flashed into my soul by the Holy Spirit, that there was nothing in the world to be done but to fall down on one's knees, and accepting the Savior and His salvation, to praise Him forevermore. Thus while my dear mother was praising God in her chamber, I was praising Him in the old warehouse to which I had gone alone to read at my leisure.

"Several days elapsed before I ventured to make my beloved sister the confidante of my joy, and then only after she had promised not to tell anyone of my soul secret. When our dear mother came home a fortnight later, I was the first to meet her at the door, and to tell her I had such glad news to give. I can almost feel that dear mother's arms around my neck, as she pressed me to her bosom and said, 'I know, my boy, I have been rejoicing in the glad tidings you have to tell me.' 'Why,' I asked in surprise, 'has Amelia broken her promise? She said she would tell no one.' My dear mother assured me that it was not from any human source that she had learned the tidings, and went on to tell me the little incident mentioned."

And so Hudson Taylor's God-directed career was assured, to be characterized by hardships and suffering, but also by blessed results in reaching needy souls. Dr. Robert E. Speer, in *Christianity and The Nations,* quotes a missions authority, F.F. Ellinwood, as saying, "Mr. Hudson Taylor, in the great missionary conference of 1900, urged the missionaries to aim at the conversion of men at once, even though it might be the first and possibly the only opportunity, and he gave instances in which the work of the Spirit had thus directly owned the message and made it effectual."

But we don't need to depend on statements of long ago to emphasize the lessons of Hudson Taylor's life. Recently Warren Wiersbe held him forth as an example for our day: "Taylor learned to pray and trust God for finances. He learned to give what he had to others, trusting God to meet his needs a day at a time. His faith in God, and sober living, saved his life when he contracted blood poisoning while in medical training in London."

Lest any think missionary life is dull, we may conclude with this excerpt from J. Gilchrist Lawson: "In 1853, Taylor was sent to China . . . The vessel he was on was nearly wrecked upon the coast of New Guinea. The passengers could see the cannibal islanders running about on the shore and preparing fires with which to cook them." But God had a man on that ship for whom He had something else in store. May God give us men of such faith and courage today.

35

REUBEN ARCHER TORREY:
Evangelist and Educator

S ome time before his death, it was announced that Dr. R. A.
Torrey would be back for one final service in the pulpit of the
Church of the Open Door in Los Angeles, the church he long
served with distinction and whose large auditorium he well-nigh
filled each Sunday. His writings having been a great help to me in
my early Christian days, I attended the service with considerable
interest and was not disappointed, as tens of thousands could have
testified of his preaching. After the service I was privileged to speak
to and shake hands with Dr. Torrey.

The Encyclopaedia Britannica (1973 edition) states of Dr.
Torrey, "U.S. evangelist, one of the successors of D. L. Moody. He
was distinguished among the other revivalists of the period by his
educational background; he graduated from Yale University . . .
studied at Leipzig and Erlangen (Germany)."

The *Wycliffe Biographical Dictionary of the Church* reports, "He
was the author of forty religious books." Again, "Between 1902 and
1906 Dr. Torrey carried on a remarkable series of evangelistic cam-
paigns of modern times, laboring in Australia, Tasmania, New
Zealand, India, China, Japan, Britain, Germany, Canada, and the
United States." Both his books and his lectures were fully abreast

of modern scholarship, but put simply enough to benefit the common man.

We take the story of his conversion from *R. A. Torrey, Apostle of Certainty,* by Roger Martin (Sword of the Lord Publishers). Even before entering college, "One of his favorite pastimes was to browse through the attic of his home where old books from the library were stored. One day he discovered one, the *Covenant of the First Presbyterian Church* in Geneva, New York, and curled up in a corner to read it. He quickly became absorbed in it. 'I wonder if I could become a church member.' He readily assented to most of the propositions in the book until he came to a portion which said that a Christian must be willing to do exactly what God wanted him to do. At this point he closed the book abruptly and cast it aside. 'If I say "yes" to that, God will just as likely call me to preach the Gospel, and I have determined to be a lawyer. I will not become a Christian.' . . .

"Torrey entered Yale at the youthful age of fifteen . . . Adept at winning card games because of his keen memory, he spent many an afternoon in this pastime. He enjoyed dancing so much that he often spent as many as four evenings a week in this entertainment. Smoking and social drinking were common habits on the Yale campus, and they held an attraction for Reuben as well. All . . . presented themselves to Reuben and he took full advantage of them . . .

"But religious exercises were also given a pronounced emphasis . . . Reuben had not yet become a Christian, but he kept up religious appearances. He regularly attended Sunday services, read his Bible and prayed daily as a matter of course. These habits had been ingrained in him from childhood, but he had never attended a religious service that made any lasting impression on him. At this juncture his strong bent toward worldly pleasure completely dominated his thinking and living . . . 'In those former days I loved the card table, the theater, the dance, the horse-race, the champagne supper, and I hated the prayer-meeting and Sunday services.' . . .

"Reuben approached the end of his junior year. He had not found the rich satisfaction he had expected in his quest at the fountain of worldly pleasure. Even his high ambition to become a lawyer had dimmed. With his 'confidence in the flesh' sadly shaken, the crisis came.

"In the middle of the night he awoke, smothered with a feeling of great despondency. Life seemed to hold no hope. In desperation he sprang from his bed to the washstand and opened the drawer. 'I am going to end this whole miserable business. Where is that razor?' But God held his trembling, fumbling fingers. And in that moment's lapse he dropped to his knees in the darkness beside the open drawer and began to pray. 'God, if You will take away this awful burden, I will preach.' Immediately a strange peace settled over him and he fell into a restful sleep.

"As he remarked subsequently, 'I had gone to bed with no more thought of becoming a Christian than I had of jumping over the moon.' There was no preliminary conviction, but afterward it came to him, 'My mother, four hundred and twenty-seven miles away was praying, and praying that I would become a minister of the Gospel. And though I had gotten over sermons and arguments and churches, and everything else, I could not get over my mother's prayers.' . . .

"He told his classmates of his decision. They thought he was joking . . . It was not until the end of his senior year at Yale that he made a public profession of faith and united with the church. His initial hesitation about uniting with the church because of his slow progress spiritually was overcome, and he decided to make an open confession of Christ."

Another work giving an account of Dr. Torrey's conversion is *Roads To Christ* by C.S. Isaacson, which concludes the conversion account with these own words of Torrey: "While in the Divinity School, largely through the influence of Gibbon, I was plunged into utter agnosticism. I determined to know the truth, whether the Bible was the Word of God or not; whether there ever was such a person as Jesus Christ, and whether He was the Son of God or not, and whether there was any God. Out of this darkness I came into the clear light of an assured faith in all the great Christian verities. From that day God has led me on every year, and I think I might almost say every day has been better than the one which preceded it."

And finally, we may quote again the words of Dr. Torrey as found in Wilbur M. Smith's *Profitable Bible Study* (p. 73). Dr. Torrey said, "The joys that come from earnest study of various kinds—philosophical, scientific, historical, literary, and linguistic—have been among my chief joys for many years, nearly my whole life through, from early boyhood, but there has come into my heart from Bible study, through digging into the gold mines of this wonderful and inexhaustible Book, a joy with which the joys that have come from all other forms of study are not worthy to be compared for one moment."

Taken from the book, R.A. Torry, *Apostle of Certainty* by Roger Martin. Copyright Sword of the Lord Publishers. Used by permission of Sword of the Lord Publishers.

36

W. CAMERON TOWNSEND:
The Word of God in Every Language

While I was teaching at John Brown University in Arkansas, during the school year 1933-34, a missionary from Central America appeared on the campus. Cameron Townsend by name, he wanted to start a summer training camp for budding missionaries. He had plans worked out where they would rough it nearby as they studied linguistics and related matters. As I was about to leave for the summer, I turned over to Brother Townsend the facilities of my otherwise vacant office. But I well remember his asking me to help get out a single sheet announcement and suggested program for that first summer camp. As assistant editor of the university paper, I recall running back and forth to the print shop in an effort to get Townsend's brochure just the way he wanted it.

When I returned after that summer, Dr. Brown, of the university, with a subdued smile on his face, remarked how Townsend, running around with a bare handful of students, seemed as happy as a hen with a few chicks (in contrast to the university's hundreds). But with his Summer Institute of Linguistics and Wycliffe Bible

Translators, Townsend surely made his mark in the world, or, as it could well be said, *upon* the world. Indeed, speaking of the upsurge of Bible translations in this century, *Eerdman's Handbook To The History Of Christianity* (p. 630) declares, "The founding of the Wycliffe Bible Translators in 1934 by an American translator, Cameron Townsend, was a milestone. Today (1977) it is the largest missionary society in the world."

Years later I was welcomed to Wycliffe's annual conference in Mexico City, following which Townsend escorted some of us to visit a few of their active centers. Many years later still, Townsend called me by long distance to report on their entering the Philippines, attributing their burden for that field to my bringing the need there to their attention. No wonder I am interested in how the Lord dealt with him in the beginning.

Townsend's early experience of Christ is told in *Uncle Cam,* by James and Marti Hefley. We read: "All his life Cam has been a man of one Book—the Bible. He recalls how every weekday morning, before milking, his father would read three chapters—five on Sunday. After breakfast came family devotions—Bible reading, a hymn, and prayers . . . He always ended his prayers with, 'May the knowledge of the Lord cover the earth as the waters cover the sea.'

"At twelve Cam joined the Presbyterian church. Will [his father] took him out to the barn and questioned him concerning his beliefs. Cam wrote down his answers for his deaf father. Will was pleased and satisfied that his son had a firm personal faith in Christ as his Lord and Savior . . .

"World War I had already flared in Europe when he enrolled in Occidental College in Los Angeles [where I enrolled a few years later]. During his sophomore year Cam was drawn to the Student Volunteer Band. New joiners had to tell why they wanted to be members. Though Cam belonged to the debating club, when his turn came he found it hard to articulate his concern for foreign missions . . .

"Once after a Bible class, a fellow student asked, 'Cameron, do you know how we're saved?'

"'By the life of Christ, I guess,' Cam replied lamely.

"His classmate looked appalled. 'No, by Christ's death! Haven't you studied the theology of the atonement?'

"'Well, no,' Cam said. 'I guess maybe I should.'"

Townsend began his missionary work in Guatemala and soon learned of the Indian tribes whom he contacted in itinerant work. At one place "he entered a sort of beer garden and offered a tract to an Indian who was drinking liquor. 'Sorry *senor*, but I cannot read,' the ragged man said. Cam smiled and walked away, but a few minutes later he heard the man's footsteps behind him. '*Amigo*, I have a friend who reads. If you will sell me a little book, *por favor?*'

"Cam handed over a Gospel and invited the Indian whose name was Tiburcio, to the believers' Sunday services. To his great joy, Tiburcio came and at the end of Cam's sermon declared himself a believer. Cam's morale jumped 1,000 percent, for this was the first person he had helped find salvation . . ." Some weeks later Cam met a friend who "told Cam that Tiburcio, his first convert, was following the Lord faithfully. 'The owner of the big ranch where he works has noticed the change in him and has made him a foreman! He is paying off his debts.' Cam was overjoyed at the news."

Townsend's burden for the Indians grew. He saw their need for Scripture they could understand—the Word of God in their own tongue. But the Central American Mission at the time questioned it. In preparation for its next general council meeting in Chicago, the mission sent Dr. Lewis Sperry Chafer, secretary of the mission, down to Guatemala (about the time Chafer was starting a seminary in Dallas).

Townsend escorted him around the Indian districts, particularly in his own Cakchiquel area. Chafer was surprised that Townsend had not had more theological training. He began questioning him, but Townsend always seemed to turn each question back to the need of the Indians. After several other attempts, Chafer asked, "What are your views on election?"

"'Oh, I believe in election all right,' said Cam. 'I also believe in my responsibility to tell the Good News to every person possible. One time two of the Cakchiquel preachers and I went to a Quiche community. Every time we would approach a group of huts where a clan lived, everybody would hide. But at one place a woman stayed out to tend the ants she was toasting in a big skillet over a campfire. I pulled out a coin and politely asked if she would sell me some. She called inside for a bowl which she filled with the Quiche delicacy. The two Cakchiquels frowned. 'We've never eaten ants,' they told me. 'Well, I haven't either, but we're going to eat some now,' I said. 'It'll be worth it if it encourages them to listen to the gospel.' And you know, it worked. While we were munching on ants the Indians began to emerge from their hiding places. They were so impressed at outsiders eating ants that they lost their fear and listened to the gospel as long as we kept eating. So one of us would preach while the other two ate. The people received a steady sermon as long as the ants lasted.

"Chafer laughed and asked Cam if, indeed, he held any strong doctrinal positions. 'Well, . . . I believe in grace. God's grace. And I want to share it with the Indians.'"

Townsend was bold and did not stop in later days in approaching even the revolutionary President of Mexico. His concern for the welfare of the Indians won favor with the anti-capitalistic President, General Cardenas (who encouraged him, stood later as best man at his wedding).

After a visit in the Townsend home, during which Cam displayed deep concern for the Indians, President Cardenas "gave a fountain pen inscribed with his name in gold letters to Cam. 'With this I have signed my documents and decrees for the past three-and-a-half years. More land has been given to peasants with it than any pen in Mexican history. I want you to have it.'"

Cam was deeply moved and with that pen he wrote a long letter to the President in which he bore a positive testimony. "Cam movingly summarized the character and life of Christ, climaxing with His death, resurrection, and presence with believers. Then he added a short personal testimony: "Mr. President, is it any wonder that I have dedicated my life to such a Friend? At least I can assure you in the most categorical way that in Him I have found everlasting joy and peace, because he has the faculty of imparting His own abundant and eternal life to His followers . . .'"

May that be the kind of witness that will always prevail!

Taken from the book, *Uncle Cam*, Copyright Wycliffe Bible Translators. Used by permission of Wycliffe Bible Translators, P.O. Box 2727, Huntington Beach, CA 92647.

37

A.W. TOZER:
A Prophet for Our Times

In Dr. A. W. Tozer's great Alliance church in Chicago, I was impressed on meeting the distinguished pastor. A gracious and condescending man, he yet conveyed the idea that he meant total business for God. He seemed to look right into the depths of the soul of one he met, yet left one feeling comfortable.

From the back cover of his biography, from which we shortly take his conversion, we read: *"Reared on a farm and as a lad limited to a one-room country school education, Doctor Tozer achieved the rank of a scholar. Such descriptive terms as oracle, seer, and Christian mystic were applied to him. In the hearts of thousands of Christians was created a thirst for the deep things of God . . . his work as prophet, scholar, mystic, theologian, pastor, missionary, poet, author, editor . . .*

"He was a preacher to preachers and college students. A weekly radio broadcast increased his influence. He was in popular demand from coast to coast. As editor of The Alliance Witness, *he gained international recognition. His editorials were published simultaneously in the United States and Great Britain. His writings were translated into more than fifteen languages."*

Dr. William Culbertson, president of the Moody Bible Institute, described Tozer as "a prophet, a man of God, his life as well as his sermons attest that fact. He thunders the message of God for those of us who are dreadfully poverty-stricken . . ." And that great missionary statesman, author and professor, Dr. Samuel Zwemer, characterized him as "a heart thirsting after God, eager to grasp at least the outskirts of His ways, the abyss of His love for sinners, and the height of His unapproachable majesty—and a busy pastor in Chicago! . . . a self-made scholar, an omnivorous reader with a remarkable library of theological and devotional books, and one who seemed to burn the midnight oil in the pursuit of God."

His biography by David J. Fant, Jr., is entitled *A. W. Tozer, A Twentieth Century Prophet.* His conversion is related as follows:

"Not always in early years was his conduct exemplary. On the slightest provocation he would pick a quarrel with neighborhood children, drawing the wrath of their mothers upon him. One day Tozer and his sister climbed an apple tree. Swinging back and forth on a high limb he burst into song: 'Is there any room in heaven for a lad like me?' A response came quickly: 'If there's going to be any room for you in heaven, you'll have to mend your ways!' and a neighbor's discerning wife emerged from the brush . . .

"Sundays on the farm were devoted to reading and, like Abraham Lincoln, Tozer availed himself of the few books at hand. At fifteen, in Akron, the artist within him began to emerge. He enrolled for cartoon lessons and showed considerable promise; the sharpness of his wit was forecast in his sketches. However, he lost all interest in this after his conversion.

"At Akron the family had opportunity for the first time to attend church, and Tozer accompanied his younger brother and sisters to Sunday school.

"And at Akron the big event happened. In 1915, shortly before his eighteenth birthday, Tozer was converted, and it was for him a transforming experience like Saul's on the road to Damascus. Certainly the results were the same, though the time and place differed. This was on a busy city street corner, with an elderly man the open-air preacher. But his words were pricks: 'If you don't know how to be saved, just call on God saying, "Lord, be merciful to me a sinner."' Tozer sought sanctuary in the attic and there wrestled with God. When he emerged he was a new creation. He joined a Methodist church and was baptized by immersion in the Church of the Brethren.

"Conversion was immediate, but as is generally the case, the seed had been planted long before. It would appear that God had laid His hand on this young man very early in life. The soil for the planting had been prepared by his paternal grandmother who often talked to the children about God.

"At once Tozer began to witness for Christ. He attached himself to his new-found friends in preaching on the streets and conducting neighborhood prayer meetings. For these he boldly rang doorbells, requesting the privilege of holding a meeting in the home.

"Only once did he miss the way. With a boyhood chum he forsook home and job, taking a small boat down the Ohio River with no particular destination in view. The boat capsized and all their possessions were lost, and he sheepishly returned to Akron. The experience was not without value, however, for it made him sympathetic with the backslider. Henceforth there was to be no wavering in his Christian life.

"As a youth he was inclined to be cynical, but as time passed, tempered by the soft breezes of the Spirit, his doubts were replaced by unshakable Christian faith.

"Conversion worked a miracle in Tozer's life; to it he traced the awakening of his intellect and every other gift, and family and friends were quick to note the difference. But the long ascent of the pilgrim walk had just begun. Character must be molded by experience; growth in grace and the knowledge of God must come. Gradually, day by day, cynicism gave way to faith, and kindness and consideration displaced a quarrelsome and argumentative spirit. Tozer was off to a fast start, and as he approached the end of the walk he said, 'I have found God cordial and generous and in every way easy to live with.'"

Taken from the book, *A. W. Tozer, a Twentieth-Century Prophet* by F. J. Fant. Copyright Christian Publications. Used by permission of Christian Publications.

38

DAWSON TROTMAN:
Apostle to Servicemen

Mounting on the back of his heavy-built motorcycle, Dawson said to me, "Get a firm grip on my 'Sam Brown' belt, for when we take off, it is sure to thrust you backward; just hang on, and you'll be all right." With a wild dash we sped off through traffic, cutting in and out of lanes as we made our way from Los Angeles to a nearby town to speak at a boy's club young Dawson sponsored. His bold, uninhibited manner was typical of his forthright service for Christ.

Dawson Trotman founded the Navigators, a Bible study and witnessing organization, originally among naval men. I came more to appreciate the Navigators upon returning to the Philippines immediately after World War II, when many of these Christian men in service attended and brought others to services in the First Baptist Church of Manila.

The following account of Dawson's conversion is largely from a narrative by Loren Sanny (director of the Navigators after Dawson perished rescuing a girl from drowning), first published in England, and from Dawson's own testimony in *Born to Reproduce* (Back to the Bible Publishers, Lincoln, Nebraska).

"Dawson's father had traveled the great West as a cowboy, married and settled in Arizona. An atheist named Dawson so profoundly influenced his life that he chose that name for his son. Singular indeed was the fact that the son so named met Christ and later proved in his own life the power of God denied by the one whose name he bore.

"In a small town near Los Angeles Dawson grew to have his father's love for adventure. Dawson says, 'I had been the president of the student body of the high school and valedictorian of the graduating class, yet I was stealing from the school funds. I joined the Boy Scouts and took the oath, but it was all on the outside. A week after I graduated from high school, I went out and got drunk.'

"It is said that often he would drive his 'Model T' Ford down the streets with the throttle wide open, steering from the back seat with his feet!

"Two months after his twentieth birthday, under the influence of liquor, Dawson was arrested and on his way to jail. He thought of his mother, ill at home, who was praying for him. She had expressed to him a fear that she would die if she ever heard he was in jail.

"The big policeman looked down at him and asked, 'Do you like this kind of life?'

"'Sir, I hate it,' he answered. The officer took him to a park and made him stay there for three hours until he sobered up. Then, with a promise to do better, the officer let him go.

"That was on a Friday night. The next Sunday he went to church.

"Dawson says, 'God picked out a couple of schoolteachers to have a large part in my coming to Christ. Miss Mills was a general science teacher, and I was one of her problem pupils. She wrote my name down on her prayer list and prayed for me every day for six solid years. On the Friday night when I was arrested, she was home with Miss Thomas, looking up verses in the Bible to find ten on the subject of salvation which they could give to the young people to memorize. Little did she know that the boy for whom she had prayed for six years was going to memorize those verses.'

"When Dawson got to church, he found the young people were having a contest in which points would be won by memorizing verses from the Bible. With a characteristic desire to win, Dawson learned the ten verses by the next Sunday night, and he was the only one to learn them all! During the next week he learned ten more. And the Word of God did its work.

"During the third week of his renewed interest in church,

Dawson was on his way to work, with the twenty verses of Scripture stored away in his memory, when something happened. He had gone back to the old way of life, frequenting the taverns on week nights, even though he attended church on Sunday. As he walked to work that day, lunch pail in hand, the truth of one of the verses he had memorized penetrated his mind in all the power of the Holy Spirit. It was John 5:24: 'Verily, verily, I say unto you, He that heareth my word, and believeth on him that sent me, hath everlasting life . . .'

"'That's wonderful,' he thought. *'Hath everlasting life!'* For the first time he prayed when he wasn't in trouble. 'O God, whatever this means, I want to have it.' Then in a flash another of the memorized verses came to mind: 'But as many as received him, to them gave he power to become the sons of God, even to them that believe on his name' (John 1:12). Immediately he responded, speaking again to God, 'Whatever it means to receive Jesus, I do it right now.' He said later, 'That was my new birth.' He did not understand what had happened, but he did know a distinct change had taken place in his life.

"Realizing a hunger for more of the Word, he began to memorize a verse a day, a practice which he continued for three years. He also began to witness to others about Christ. Memorization of Scripture for the purpose of victory and growth had a great champion in this young man who had seen its remarkable power in his life."

39

MEL TROTTER:
Rescue Mission Pioneer

I well remember Mel Trotter—not tall, but as a heavy-set man who moved not easily—but with deliberation. I was privileged to hear him give a series of lectures on rescue mission work, of which he was considered the most knowledgeable of anyone in America at that time, having been instrumental in establishing some 66 rescue missions in leading cities of our land. I recall him saying at the outset that to be an effective rescue mission worker one did not have to be a converted bum as he was. I also heard him give his personal testimony more than once. His conversion was, indeed, a marvelous tribute to the life-transforming power of the gospel and has become a classic example of the great change wrought by regeneration.

The story of Mel Trotter is told in his autobiography, *These Forty Years;* in *Mel Trotter, A Biography,* by Fred C. Zarfas; and in *The Pacific Garden Mission,* by Carl F.H. Henry (Zondervan).

"In his youth Mel considered an education unnecessary to success. His parents did their best to get him to go to school, but he was more interested in his father's saloon and the gambling den down the street. He skipped school more often than he attended it.

"Mel followed in his father's footsteps. Early in life he learned the taste of liquor and, like his father, became a drunkard, and his brothers with him.

"After he was saved, Mr. Trotter many times made the statement: 'I didn't get a very good start in the first place, for my job was tending bar in my father's saloon. Booze got the best of me pretty early in life, and before I was twenty years old I was the common drunkard of our town.'

"He used to say, 'I followed the horses for a time and knew the pedigree of every race horse in the country. I got to know a great deal about four-legged trotters. I was always stuck on the finest horses. I kept on drinking, and the first thing I knew, I couldn't stop.

"One day I would be flat broke and maybe the next I would have a roll big enough to choke a cow. I have also seen the time when I sold my shoes to buy whiskey. One day I would be rolling in money, but the next day I'd be panhandling for a flop [floor space enough to sleep on].'

"Since he had acquired the taste for drink back in his father's saloon, it was easy for the devil to lead him for ten hideous years into the depths of drunken hopelessness and stupidity. Mel despised himself for his weakness and again and again begged for his wife's forgiveness and promised never to touch liquor again. But each promise was followed by another drunken spree.

"Disaster struck at the little Trotter homestead one wintry, snowy night. They had been out visiting neighbors and had just returned home. Mrs. Trotter went into the house while her husband put the horse up in the barn for the night. After awhile, when he did not come in, she became anxious and went out to see where he was. When she got to the barn, she discovered that Mel had left, taking the horse and buggy with him. A dreadful fear gripped her heart.

"Years after, when telling about this experience, he said, 'I drove the horse and buggy to town, put them in the shed behind the saloon, and going into the saloon I said to the gang gathered there, "There's the old nag and buggy out there. The drinks are on me. Everyone have something to drink. Drink up the horse!" Hours later I staggered the eleven miles home drunk—and minus the horse and buggy.'

"'I even committed burglary to satisfy the awful craving for drink. God gave us only one baby. When the little fellow was hardly two years old, I went one day after a ten-day's drunk to find my wife in our cold, bare home, if you could call it a home, and found our boy dead in his mother's arms. I'll never forget that day. I looked at that little fellow and then at his heartbroken mother, and I could think of only one thing: I said, "I'm a murderer! I can't stand it, and I won't stand it. I'll end my life!'"

"Unable to work, and not sober long enough to hold down a job if he could, he was reduced to a place where respectability and decency fled, and he was left an abject specimen of manhood, ragged, shoeless, and penniless. His dirt-begrimed body filled him with disgust.

"It was winter, and snow lay on the ground. Not long since, he had sold his shoes to get another drink. His feet seemed like lumps of lead, and with every step rapier-like pains pierced his body. A few hours before, Mel had dropped off a boxcar as it rolled into the yards of Chicago. It was January, and a bitter cold was sweeping in from Lake Michigan. Wearily he dragged himself along the streets. There was no comfort nor warmth for Mel. There! It flashed into his drink-sodden mind again. End it all tonight—jump in the lake, *jump in the lake*. He was too numb with cold and too lonely and sick to care.

"Telling the story of his conversion, he would say, 'I was kicked out of a Clark Street (Chicago) saloon dead drunk, broke, no shoes on my feet and almost no clothes on my back. I was headed for Lake Michigan, intending to end it all on the advice of the bartender who had kicked me out.'

"Tom, ex-jockey and former faro-dealer (card sharp), was on the job outside the Pacific Garden Mission on old Van Buren Street that momentous night. When Tom took his stand outside the mission, he was tempted to go inside where it was warm. It had been cold all day with a blizzard raging, but Tom's heart was warm and his eye keen.

"At that moment a few blocks away a ragged bum staggered up the street on his way to the lake. The ex-jockey soul winner saw him coming. Never did he have stronger urge to leave his post of duty and get off the cold street into the warm mission where a gospel service was in progress.

"The slouching form came to an abrupt stop. A friendly hand was placed upon his shoulder; a cheery voice sounded in his ear. Stupidly drunk, Mel was unable to comprehend anything. Tom pushed him through the doors into the mission. A vacant chair stood over by the chimney. Tom shoved him into it, whereupon the poor wretch leaned his head against the wall and went to sleep.

"Later in the service Mel stirred, then opened his eyes. Where was he? The last he remembered he was on his way to drown himself in Lake Michigan. It finally dawned on him that he was in a religious meeting. Something pierced his heart and mind. He brushed his ragged sleeves across his brow. He shook his head in a vain attempt to blot out the memory there.

"At the close of the service Harry Monroe said, 'Jesus loves you, and so do I; put up your hand for prayer, let God know you want to make room for Him in your heart.' Mel Trotter raised his hand, rose to his feet, and staggered to the altar. Mr. Monroe got down on his knees beside that human derelict and, putting his arm around his shoulders, told him the story of God's redeeming love. When Harry finished telling him the way of hope and salvation, Mel cried out for mercy and forgiveness, and God for Christ's sake saved his soul. When God heard drunken Trotter's cry for help and salvation that night, He not only saved him, but He also broke the fetters which bound him. He never touched another drop of liquor from that time; he never wanted to.

"A little later a man stood to his feet, still clothed in rags, penniless, dirty and dishevelled, but a heavenly light shone on his face, and a smile that thousands saw in the years that followed. One of Heaven's greathearts stood right there that night, one of America's leading evangelists, one of the most used and successful mission men of all time. That man was Mel Trotter.

"In his new-found joy Mel had to tell practically everyone he met about it; every drunkard he met on the streets, old or young, white or black, and many believed him and followed him on the Jesus way. The erstwhile drunkard and bum still walked along skid row, but it no longer held any terrors for him. 'Nightmare Alley' became 'Sunshine Lane.'"

———

Taken from the book, *Mel Trotter* by Fred C. Zarfas. Copyright ©1950 by Zondervan Publishing House. Used by permission of Zondervan Publishing House.

40

GEORGE W. TRUETT:
Southern Baptist Giant

In graduate study in Dallas, Texas, I used to go often to hear George W. Truett at the First Baptist Church of that city. What a dynamic, heart-searching preacher he was! Nothing light or frivolous about him, and yet he knew how to make his sermons interesting and hold one's attention. He always presented Christ and the gospel in its saving power.

Of Truett, the *Wycliffe Biographical Dictionary of the Church* says in part, "entered pastorate in the First Baptist Church of Dallas with seven hundred members, and continued in the same church until his death forty-seven years later, leaving the congregation with a membership of seventy-eight hundred. One of the greatest preachers of his day and a great evangelist. His influence reached far beyond congregation or his city."

Indeed, under Truett that church grew to be the largest Baptist church in the world. While so recognized in Dallas, his ministry was world-wide. Probably no other single preacher had the privilege of ministering in so many countries as did Dr. Truett—and all before the days of easy air travel. He preached in England, Scotland, Wales, Sweden, France, Germany, Switzerland, Latvia, Poland, Hungary, Romania, Palestine, Egypt, India, Burma, Singapore, China, Japan, Brazil, Argentina, Uruguay, Chile, Peru, and other lands! He went to Europe during World War I, enduring the dangers of the front, where his usual schedule consisted of six addresses a day, beside conferences and personal interviews.

Apparently Dr. Truett was too busy to give much attention to preparing his sermons for publication, but they found their way into print and were greatly used. His first volume of sermons appeared in 1915 and went through seventeen printings. As a young minister I secured his volume of sermons, *A Quest For Souls,* found them to be ideal models both as to structure and content, took the book to the mission field and back, and have long cherished it.

Early in his ministry in Dallas, a tragic hunting accident occurred when Dr. Truett's hammerless gun went off as he was shifting his position, shooting his good friend, the Dallas Chief of Police and a member of his church. The Chief lingered for a day or two, but succumbed in the hospital. The whole city was shocked. Dr. Truett was utterly crushed, heartbroken, he could hardly sleep or eat for a week. He nearly gave up the ministry—a man of less fortitude would have. But it proved a turning point in his life, bringing out the best in him. It left its mark, however, and Dr. Truett was said never to give way to laughter again in public. A greater turning point, only, was his conversion to God when nineteen years of age.

George Truett grew up in a southern mountain home in North Carolina, where good influences held a large place, including good books. Among the volumes he became acquainted with were Bunyan's *Pilgrim's Progress,* Foxe's *Book of Martyrs,* Baxter's *Saints Everlasting Rest,* and the sermons of Spurgeon and Moody. Family, wholesome, associates and faithful ministers of the gospel likewise played an important role in his early life.

Annual two-week revival meetings were held in his home church, and by the time he was able to take in their significance he was deeply impressed by them. Even at the age of six, he later reported, he became conscious of a real need for God's forgiveness while listening to a country preacher in such a series. After getting home at night he wished for someone to tell him how to get right with God. Again at the age of eleven very much the same experience was repeated.

Finally, when nineteen, during a one-week series of meetings, the preacher came to what was supposed to be his farewell sermon at the Sunday morning service. At the regular Sunday evening service, however, the same preacher walked in with the pastor and it was explained that a deep sense of need being felt, the revivalist postponed his next meeting for a week. This made a deep impression upon the congregation.

That evening the preacher took as his text, "Now the just shall live by faith: but if any draw back, my soul shall have no pleasure in him" (Hebrews 10:38). Faith in Christ as imperative was set forth—faith in a Redeemer mighty to save; then the peril of a soul drawing back upon being faced with the call of Christ; and finally came a stirring appeal to accept that Savior by simple and immediate faith, and to publicly demonstrate it.

A large number responded and among those who went forward was young George Truett, glad to make his decision known before the congregation, embracing Christ and His salvation.

At home during the night he pondered the claim of Christ upon his life. If the Lord should demand his all—total commitment for life—would he be willing? After pondering it, he responded in the affirmative, ready to pay whatever price might be involved. Then a great peace settled over him and sound rest ensued. In the morning he confided this experience to his mother, who sympathized fully, and they rejoiced together.

Although teaching in a country school all day, the next night he was back in the service at the little country church. When opportunity was given for folks to tell their "Christian experience," George readily responded, giving positive testimony to his faith in Christ and new-found joy.

At the following Wednesday night meeting, at its conclusion, the pastor did an unexpected thing which took Truett utterly by surprise. The house crowded to the doors, he suddenly called upon young George to appeal to the people regarding their need to respond to the Savior and accept the proffered salvation. At once George did so, pleading earnestly and with passion in such a way it made a deep impression and bore fruit. After he had finished, however, George felt ashamed and thought he had made a fool of himself. But it was his mother, again, who showed understanding and assured him. So George Truett was on his way toward a life of usefulness in the kingdom of God.

During the summer of 1938, six years before his death and following more than forty years as pastor in Dallas, Truett suffered a severe illness. Becoming delirious, he was rushed by ambulance to Baylor Hospital where he was confined for a month. His wife remained by his side day and night. Later she bore this witness: "All through his unconsciousness and delirium from fever or medicine, his subconscious mind was just as clean and Christian as his daily life has always been . . . In his delirium he was quoting Scripture, preaching, calling men to Christ or praying for them. A great revelation of the real man."